# CHRIST AND

*Understanding the events at the end of the century and recognizing our tasks*

Peter Tradowsky

TEMPLE LODGE
London

Translated by John M. Wood

The material in this volume is based on lectures given in recent years under the auspices of the Anthroposophical Society in Kleebach, Berlin, Dresden, Leipzig, Rostock and Weimar

Temple Lodge Publishing
51 Queen Caroline Street
London W6 9QL

Published by Temple Lodge 1998

Originally published in German under the title *Christ und Antichrist, Von den Erkenntnis-aufgaben für das Jahrhundertende* by Verlag am Goetheanum, Dornach, Switzerland in 1996

© Verlag am Goetheanum 1996
This translation © Temple Lodge Publishing 1998

The moral right of the author has been asserted under the Copyright, Designs and Patents Act, 1988

All rights reserved. No part of this publication may be reproduced, stored in a retrieval system, or transmitted, in any form or by any means, electronic, mechanical, photocopying, recording or otherwise, without the prior permission of the publishers

A catalogue record for this book is available from the British Library

ISBN 0 904693 94 5

Cover by Studio MAOSS. Illustrations by William Blake: 'The Number of the Beast is 666' (1805) and 'Soldiers Casting Lots for Christ's Garments' (1800)

Typeset by DP Photosetting, Aylesbury, Bucks
Printed and bound in Great Britain by Cromwell Press Limited, Broughton Gifford, Wiltshire

## Contents

| | | |
|---|---|---|
| 1 | The Problem Stated | 1 |
| 2 | How Can We Distinguish Between Different Evil Beings? | 6 |
| 3 | The Description of Sorath | 12 |
| 4 | The Encounter with the Apocalyptic Beast, the Year 1933 | 23 |
| 5 | Sorath Raises his Head at the End of the Century | 48 |
| | His changed method of working since 1933 | 48 |
| | The War of All against All | 50 |
| | What must be achieved by the year 2000? | 53 |
| | How is Sorath's activity revealed? | 56 |
| | The tragedy of the Threefold Social Order as the form appropriate to Christ | 64 |
| | Mammon and Halley's Comet (1910/1986) | 68 |
| | Ahriman's forthcoming incarnation | 73 |
| 6 | Coming to Terms with the Apocalyptic Beast | 79 |
| 7 | The Christ Event of the Twentieth Century | 91 |
| | Notes | 101 |

'The night seems deeper now to press around me,
But in my inmost spirit all is light.'

Goethe: *Faust*, Part II, Act V, 'Midnight'.

# 1
# *The Problem Stated*

The present work is intended to elucidate two statements—only made known in 1991—in which Rudolf Steiner posed questions connected with the year 1933 and the end of the century. At the same time, the considerations dealt with in my book *Ere the Century Closes* will be revived, continued and pursued in greater depth. Both statements by Rudolf Steiner come from the last year of his outward activity, in September 1924, shortly before his illness. The first to be cited here assigns a unique position to the year 1933.

> My dear friends, in 1933 there would have been the possibility that the earth, with all that lives on it, could have been wiped out if another, wise and incalculable influence were not to come into effect—for calculations cannot always be right when comets assume their other form. We can say, as the writer of the Apocalypse would put it, that before the Etheric Christ can be properly understood by people, humanity must have passed through the encounter with the Beast, which will make its appearance in 1933...[1]

One must bring to mind what is contained in this statement. The destruction of the earth, which would have occurred according to calculated prediction, is saved from destruction by the incalculability of the comets, which Rudolf Steiner once called the 'freedom-heroes of the cosmos'.[2]

The second statement makes a connection between the end of the century and the greatest activity of Sorath:

> At the end of the century we come to the time when Sorath again raises his head most powerfully from the surrounding flood of evolution. He will oppose the vision

of Christ which will appear in the etheric world to those who are prepared to receive it in the first half of the twentieth century...[3]

Common to both statements is the connection made between the greatest event of the twentieth century, the appearance of Christ in the etheric world, and the activity of Sorath. There are two aspects to this connection of which we can become aware.

To begin with, we must evolve the necessary clarity about this universal happening to know that it is the Christ Himself who gives the impulse to evolution and that it is from Him that the initiative proceeds. Christ is not the One who gives the answers, but He who questions. The question is directed to mankind and in mankind's search for the answers Sorath intervenes with all his might as the direct opponent of Christ. It is the Parousia, the advent of the Etheric Christ, which occasions the crisis of mankind. That is the cause of the crisis.[4] One's attitude towards every happening depends ultimately on whether this truth can be retained in one's consciousness in face of the events. Experience shows that it seldom can, for the crisis, which is an experience common to all mankind, can be traced back to a multiplicity of factors, of which the common one is that no mention is ever made of the cause here cited. The innumerable outer and inner catastrophes are borne by mankind, it is true—and also by the earth itself. But in their apocalyptic character they are not seen as an outcome, but as an ultimately incomprehensible stroke of fate.[5] And all must actually remain not understandable until we become aware of the questions being asked by the approaching Christ: How do you stand towards Me in your inmost self? How do you stand in relation to My Kingdom, that is, to the spiritual world and the beings who dwell therein? The person of the twentieth century is unable to take these questions into his consciousness. In order that he shall be awakened to what is new in evolution, his existence is shaken to its very depths.

The deeper reason, however, for the ever-spreading fear in the soul is the fact that the true cause of the crisis is not understood and, tragically enough, cannot be understood in the present-day consciousness which is opposed to the spirit. The crisis demands an unavoidable decision which will lead the evolution of man and the earth in a new direction. The seriousness of its character is thought of as a help towards making this decision, but it is usually experienced more like a 'Last Judgment' in the sense of a punishment. This ultimately inappropriate impression is a result of the fear awakened by the unconscious and unexplained contrast between the approaching spiritual reality and that of existing conditions.

The second aspect of Rudolf Steiner's remarks here quoted lies in the fact that the encounter with the apocalyptic Beast has to *precede* the understanding of the Etheric Christ. Let me repeat that startling sentence, which cannot be overemphasized: 'Before the Etheric Christ can be properly understood by people, humanity must have passed through the encounter with the Beast, which will make its appearance in 1933...' To contribute towards the understanding of this sentence is one of the main aims of this book.

To begin with one must keep in mind that the task which is here undertaken has been very little understood or fulfilled. It is true that there are various writings that deal with the subject from the one or other aspect, but these creditable efforts have—according to my observation—never led in any way to a sufficiently large number of people getting to grips with this spiritual event in a serious and effective way.[6] That is not meant as a reproach, it is only intended to describe the fact that a resistance of soul is evident which prevents us from recognizing the connection that Rudolf Steiner makes. One can see that on the one hand people are willing to accept the new Christ Event. But on the other hand they are constantly compelled through the destiny of our age to cast a glance at the activity of the adversary. To see both points of view in their necessary interconnection is certainly something which still has to be accomplished. One will have to consciously overcome the fear of doing this which manifests in the soul. This conquest, which is a kind of soul probation, is necessary in order for us to stand independently within the course of events.

The spiritual rule that underlies this statement is also described by Rudolf Steiner in his lectures *From Symptom to Reality in Modern History*:

> Today when Christ is destined to appear again in the etheric body, when a kind of Mystery of Golgotha is to be experienced anew, evil will have a significance akin to that of birth and death for the fourth post-Atlantean epoch! In the fourth epoch the Christ-impulse was born out of the forces of death for the salvation of mankind. We can say that we owe the new impulse that permeated mankind to the event on Golgotha. Thus by a strange paradox mankind is led to a renewed experience of the Mystery of Golgotha in the fifth epoch through the forces of evil. Through the experience of evil it will be possible for the Christ to appear again, just as He appeared in the fourth post-Atlantean epoch through the experience of death.[7]

Whereas in the first statement we are told how to deal with the situation, in this one we are told of the experience, that is, of something which applies to man's whole being, his understanding, his feeling and his 'grasp' in the sense of coming to terms with things. Experience in the threefoldness of man does not mean just confronting something, but getting to know it within oneself without succumbing to evil. The 'distance', so to speak, is not brought about by outward means but inwardly through the experience itself by a continuing process of recognition and decision making. These processes gradually bring about a change in man which enables him to accept the new Christ revelation. Rudolf Steiner refers especially to this in the sentence: 'Thus by a strange paradox mankind is led to a renewed experience of the Mystery of Golgotha in the fifth epoch through the forces of evil.' Once again paradox can be seen as a category of spirituality, but the paradox nature of events must be taken up consciously otherwise one would not dare to fully enter into them.

The stating of these spiritual rules in *From Symptom to Reality* refers to evil in general, not to Sorath in particular. But one should not overlook the fact that dealing with this 'encounter with the Beast' is only the climax. To deal with it demands one's whole strength and this encounter is far more than just experiencing it. The specific quality of the twentieth century lies precisely in what is expressed in these words. By passing over into the 'Age of Light' mankind is exposed to evil in a way never before experienced, in order that he may be enabled to find the good. One could also say that the veil that formerly concealed the spiritual world has been torn aside and that thereby the spiritual beings work directly, unadorned and unreservedly upon human beings. This new and singular situation has, until now, only been recognized and penetrated by man's consciousness to a very slight degree. But for the present time and on into the future everything depends upon whether the problem of experiencing and dealing with evil can be solved.

# 2
# How Can We Distinguish Between Different Evil Beings?

When a person is able to differentiate, then his ego develops alertness and independence in the comprehension of objects and events. The development of the ability to perceive differences is indispensable if one's ego is to be present in the spiritual world without becoming hopelessly lost in the general impression. The recognition of evil requires more than usual perspicuity, for the evil beings have an intense desire to remain incognito. For that reason every stand against evil starts with a true assessment; the act of assessing or naming is the first line of defence.

We shall now define the elementary but little observed difference in the strength of the various evil beings. Rudolf Steiner replied as follows to the question about the difference between luciferic and ahrimanic or mephistophelean beings:

> The latter have a stronger, more powerful will towards evil. The two kinds of beings derive from different Hierarchies. At the beginning of evolution, these beings were more similar to one another; then we had retrograde beings. The stages of development overlap. The ahrimanic beings remain at a lower stage in the realm of evil and recruit new members from a variety of Hierarchies; some, for instance, remained behind on the Sun, others on the Moon. The ones which remained behind on the Sun are able to make up on the Moon for what had been missed; those which had remained behind on the Moon were able to make up for it on the Earth, and so on. Mephistophelian or ahrimanic beings are those which are

## HOW CAN ONE DISTINGUISH EVIL BEINGS?

at a higher, or also lower, level than the luciferic ones; they get new recruits from the ranks of beings ranging from Archangels to Mights (Dynamis).[8]

The question of the Asuras which follows from this is dealt with very concisely as follows: 'The Asuras—those which are evil—are beings which again stand one degree higher in their evil capacities than the ahrimanic ones and two degrees higher than the luciferic ones.'[9]

The question concerning Sorath's character, which is of particular interest here, will not be discussed in this connection, but will be gone into in greater detail in the next chapter. If one looks at the increasing degree of evil intention—Lucifer, Ahriman, Asuras—the question could arise as to whether the being of Sorath, as the Sun Demon, the direct opponent of Christ, is still more intensely filled with evil intent.

In searching for an answer to this question, another point of view might be of help, namely, the question about the starting-points of the activities of the evil powers in the being of man. The evil Asuras are beings which took part on Ancient Saturn in the creation of the physical body, which was prepared from the very start to be the bearer of the ego. In particular, man's senses were implanted as gateways into the world for the ego. During Earth evolution the consciousness soul evolved out of the physical body through a process of transformation. By that it is evident that the terrible forces of the Asuras work destructively upon the body in so far as the will is concerned, on the senses in respect of the ego and on the consciousness soul in its spiritual nature. They attack the ego by eroding the ego-bearer.

For these asuric spirits will cause what has been seized hold of by them, namely, the very core of man's being, the consciousness soul, together with the 'I', to unite with earthly materiality. Fragment after fragment will be torn out of the 'I', and in the same measure in which the asuric spirits establish themselves in the consciousness soul, man must leave parts of his existence behind on the earth. What becomes the prey of the asuric powers will be irretrievably lost. Not that the human being in his entirety will necessarily become their victim—but parts of his spirit will be torn away by the Asuric powers.[10]

Since remaining behind on the Ancient Sun, the ahrimanic beings have been engaged in forming the etheric body, through which the intellectual and sentient souls evolved. Because of that Ahriman has a great affinity to these members of man's being, upon which he makes his influence felt.

The luciferic beings were the last to unite with man's evolution. Their activity is weakest of all. They have only been connected with evolution since the astral body came into being on the Old Moon and they remained behind in their development.

If one sees where this leads, it becomes plain that Sorath appears as an isolated being who is connected with Earth evolution in so far as the ego has been implanted into man's being. The ego is a creation of the Elohim, whose leader is Christ as Logos. Thus it is that the ego is the source of love, of development and of transformation. But through world-ordained necessity the adversary rises up to negate it with the greatest power. In so far as Christ confronts the Antichrist as the hostile Sun Demon, Sorath has to be regarded as the direct opponent of the human 'I'. His evil effect on the youngest member of man's being can be looked upon as the most intense because, being the fourth step in cosmic evolution, it has jurisdiction over the future. But the key part in all this is played by the 'I' in its unfolding development; for by taking up the Christ-impulse into itself, the further cosmic/earthly evolution is introduced. Therefore it is understandable that whoever objects to this taking place will direct his whole strength in trying to prevent it.

Four evil principles are here brought into connection with the course of cosmic evolution, with the 'I' and with its three sheaths, as well as with the changes they undergo. But let me expressly state that although these are important aspects they are by no means the only ones. What must be especially taken into account is the overlapping and interpenetration of the bad and the good spiritual beings.

At the present day the question of black magic comes very much to the fore owing to the activity of the Asuras, as also of Sorath. It is characteristic of the situation that black magical practices and rituals of every description have a great attraction as an expression of resignation with regard to the activity of the 'I'. We have to ask what influence do black magicians have in public life and in politics, and, above all, what defence do we have against black magicians. The answer Rudolf Steiner gives is impressively simple:

> The best way is to try to preserve one's freedom, to use one's common sense and to make use of one's reasoning. If one is always conscious of that, one will not be in any danger and one will have no difficulties to encounter on that account. Certainly, however, as belief in authority is so prevalent nowadays and the craze to make use of a dimmed state of consciousness for recognition of all sorts of things, it would be quite likely that black magical forces might gain entry.[11]

Nobody will delude himself over the fact that what is a protection against black magic is at the same time the obvious weak spot in modern mankind. For who can find the strength to preserve his freedom in face of the spirit of our time, the present trends, the influence on the masses by the media? Where is sound judgement? Who does not see how common sense is often scorned? How many people are ready to let themselves be guided by all possible, or impossible, authorities simply in order to avoid the discomfort of having to make up their own minds? Guru worship, as the shadow-picture of ego-development, is prevalent throughout society! It is not bright and clear consciousness which is the general characteristic of mankind, but in place of the needed expansion of mind a regression of our faculties takes place, leading to unconsciousness, and the trapdoor opens to let in black-magical effects. It is not only drugs of all kinds which play their part, but also a renunciation of common sense, a loss of faith in the ways of thought by which mankind is able to arrive at the truth by scientific means.

This discernment can also be imparted in a rather strange way by Mephisto himself. After the latter had sealed a pact in blood with Faust, he was able to confuse him in his consciousness and thinking. When Faust was not present, Mephisto was able to utter his truth in triumph and without embarrassment:

> Reason and Knowledge only thou despise
> The highest strength in man that lies!
> Let but the Lying Spirit bind thee,
> And I shall have thee fast and sure!
>
> Goethe, *Faust*, Part I, 2nd study scene

The words of truth of Mephisto can act as a spur to us to follow further the path of reason and science. The scientific consciousness of the present day is certainly not ultimately a gift of Mephisto, but from it can proceed what overcomes him. For this consciousness contains in its thinking, even though sketchily and feebly to begin with, that 'highest strength' which Mephisto rightly fears. Through the spiritual content of anthroposophy, which bears within itself in the form of ideas the processes and beings of the spiritual world, it is possible to awaken the slumbering 'highest strength', to extend consciousness and to strengthen thinking. Science which progresses to become spiritual science frightens Mephisto; it is he who wants it to be despised. It is with the greatest anxiety that we observe how, just at the critical moment of the present day, trust in the development of the 'highest strength' through spirit fertilization is destroyed. But man is only able to establish himself independently in the spiritual world in a fruitful and healthy way by treading the path of spiritual science, by continually taking up the spiritual content of anthroposophy into his thoughts, so that they penetrate his whole being.[12]

# 3
# The Description of Sorath

There are three distinct steps in Rudolf Steiner's description of Sorath.[13] Knowledge of this being is widened and deepened as one follows the path which Steiner takes; but although these three stages can be followed in his work, this does not mean that they were revealed to him at the time he spoke of each.

The first comprehensive description is to be found in the *Apocalypse* cycle (Nuremberg, 1908). In this cycle Sorath is placed in the widest possible setting, namely, in the whole of evolution from Ancient Saturn to Vulcan, in the middle of which Earth evolution and the Christ Event take place. Steiner describes the evolutionary stages of Earth, in which preparation is made for an event of the far future. No mention is yet made of a specific historical context, if we disregard a general reference to the whole of post-Atlantean development, including the Mystery of Golgotha.

It is just this historical dimension which Rudolf Steiner elaborates in his *Three Streams in the Evolution of Mankind*, where he explains that the historic moment and actual date of the Mystery of Golgotha is of decisive importance for the further course of events.[14] The being of Sorath with its adversarial nature is actively engaged in post-Christian times.

But only in the last period of Rudolf Steiner's activity on earth, in September 1924, did he give utterance to the connection of Sorath with the twentieth century, as was quoted in Chapter 1. There it is specifically the year 1933 which is mentioned — at that time prophetically — and further the year 1998, both of which are of particular importance. To begin with, the first two stages of Rudolf Steiner's description will be examined in greater detail.

It must be expressly stated that Sorath's nature is an

integral part of the *Apocalypse* cycle and can only be understood in that context. Sorath's activity in connection with Earth evolution is apparent at first in three places, whereby we should take account of the fact that: 'Everything connected with the future is already being prepared at the present day.'[15] When Earth evolution has come to an end, that is to say, when the earth will have become spiritualized, those in whom the Christ has truly been taken up will be able to share in this spiritualization through the power of Christ.

'The only exception will be those who refused to take up the Christ-principle; this refusal we have to understand as a malevolent and unintelligent spiritual opposition energetically exercised.'[16]

A similar process will take place before the Earth and Sun unite once more. Those who are connected with Christ will be raised to the Sun-existence by Him who is the Sun Spirit, who became the Genius of the Earth through the Mystery of Golgotha.

Another familiar name for Christ is 'The Lamb of God'.

But there is also an opposing principle to the Lamb: there is the Sun Demon, the so-called Demon of the Sun, that which works in the evil forces of man, thrusting back the force of the Lamb. It works in such a way that a certain portion of the human race will be excluded from the evolution leading to the Sun. These are the opposing forces to the Sun, they are in opposition to the Sun.[17]

Considerably closer in Earth evolution, but historically still fairly distant, namely, at the end of the sevenfold post-Atlantean evolution, the activity of Sorath will be revealed in the 'War of All against All'. This War of All against All is an expression of misguided ego-development. Obsession with the 'I' finally leads to downfall and destruction.

The number 666 (read 6–6–6), which denotes the Beast with the two horns of the Apocalypse, presents a particular problem. Two solutions are offered. On the one hand all the cycles of world evolution from the point of view of spiritual science can be expressed in numbers, as they were in the Mysteries. As cycles of seven are involved, the end of evolution can be denoted as 777. The present stage of development can also be interpreted in this way. Saturn, Sun and Moon evolutions have been completed — that is, three of the seven planetary evolutions have come to an end. In Earth evolution the Hyberborean, Polarian, Lemurian and Atlantean epochs are four. During the present post-Atlantean age the Indian, Ancient Persian, Egypto-Chaldean, Graeco-Roman, that is again four, have been accomplished. The present state, therefore, is 344 (three–four–four). From this one can judge how far away is 666. But in connection with the Sun Demon who is active in the evil forces in man and who stands in opposition to the Sun it is expressly stated: 'At the same time they are the forces which have the tendency to be entirely thrown out of our evolution when the 666 evolutionary conditions have passed by; they will then finally be cast into the abyss.'[18] In this way the present is connected with the far distant future. It must be mentioned that human beings who have come into the clutches of the evil forces will always have the possibility of redemption in the course of time.

The other explanation of the number 666 refers to the being of man and at the same time reveals the previously hidden name of Sorath:

> What must the number 666 mean if it is to express what we have explained? It must mean the principle which leads man to complete hardening in external physical life, so that he thrusts from him all that enables him to strip off the lower principles and to rise to the higher. That which man has obtained as physical body, etheric body, astral body and lower 'I', before it rises to the higher — these four principles are already expressed by these four let-

ters, by Samech, the physical body; Vau, the etheric body; Resh, the astral body and Tau, the lower 'I'. Thus we see that the hardened aspect of these four principles, before they begin their divine evolution, is expressed by the four letters. The writer of the Apocalypse can truly say, 'Let him who hath understanding consider the number 666.'

And now we will read it. We read it in this way — reversed, of course, from right to left:

| 400 | 200 | 6 | 60 |
|-----|-----|---|-----|
| ת | ר | ו | ס |
| Tau | Resh | Vau | Samech |

We have then to supply the vowels and it reads: 'Sorath'. Sorath is the name of the Sun Demon, the adversary of the Lamb. Every such spiritual being was described not only by name but also by a certain symbolic sign. For Sorath, the Sun Demon, there was this sign:

a thick stroke bent back upon itself and terminating in two curved points.[19]

It is in this way that Rudolf Steiner characterizes Sorath — named by him for the first time — as the arch-enemy of all development and as the denier of all change. The human being who is unable to take up the Christ-principle of love into his 'I' will of necessity go this way. By 666 is also indicated the strong will of Sorath to prevent evolution from attaining to its goal of 777. This is the real seat of the tremendous opposition to ego-development. The trapdoor has to be watched through which the sorathic powers are able to snatch mankind.

'Man himself cannot be the adversary of Christ, he can only let slip the opportunity to take the Christ-principle into himself, through what dwells in him as false power. But there is such an adversary, the Sun Demon. This appears as soon as there is something that can become its prey.'[20]

The special power of seduction exercised by Sorath relates to the misuse of spiritual powers, as can already be seen at the present day and will be discussed later.

For man to be led merely into what is immoral, what is already known to normal man, did not need this monster which appears as the Sun Demon. Only when that which in a good sense distinguishes the beings who bring salvation to the human race, only when spiritual upliftment is turned to its opposite, only when spiritual power is placed in the service of the lower 'I' principle, can it bring humanity to the point when the Beast represented with two horns gains power over it! The misuse of spiritual forces is connected with that seductive power of the Beast with the two horns. And we call this abuse of the spiritual power black magic, in contradistinction to its right use, which is white magic.[21]

Out of the activity of Sorath also comes what will lead to a division in the unity of mankind. That is consciously stressed here, because in view of the events of the twentieth century the impression can arise that this process is already beginning.

Thus through the splitting up of the human race there is prepared at the same time the power to attain ever more spiritual conditions on the one hand, and thereby to obtain the use of the spiritual forces, and arrive at white magic; while on the other hand abuse of spiritual forces is a preparation for the most fearful kind of power of the two-horned Beast—black magic. Ultimately mankind will become divided into those who use white magic and those who use black magic. Thus in the mystery of 666, or Sorath, is hidden the secret of black magic; and the one who tempts us to black magic, that most fearful crime in the Earth evolution, with which no other crimes can be compared, this seducer is represented by the writer of the Apocalypse as the two-horned Beast.[22]

Rudolf Steiner opens up quite different perspectives of the being of Sorath through the results of his spiritual investigation, which he spoke about in Dornach on 11 October 1918. There he considers the question of how the present state of the consciousness soul has come about, which has lost sight of both the real approach to nature (his present view of it only presents him with a ghostlike reality) and the view of his own being. Man has the experience—albeit unconsciously—of his own being, but is unable to grasp it consciously. The answer to this question leads to an astonishing and staggering statement. Sorath was planning a devastating attack on humanity for the year AD 666, at the time of the intellectual-soul development. This was to have endowed mankind prematurely with the gift of the consciousness soul. It is easy to see that such a gift as this would have had fatal consequences. It would not only have resulted in the development of the intellectual soul being severely impeded, but the gift of the consciousness soul would have made the work of the ego superfluous. The attack was therefore directed against the 'I' as the source of development.

The dimensions which the realization of this intention would have had were clearly explained by the following words of Rudolf Steiner:

Man will have to progress to spirit-self, life-spirit, spirit-man; and of this possibility he would have been absolutely deprived. He would have remained at the stage of the consciousness soul; he would have been able to receive what the earth could give him but never go on to the Jupiter, Venus and Vulcan evolutions. (...) But then it would have been all over with him; he would have developed no further. He would have drawn this knowledge into his consciousness soul, would have placed it all with the utmost egoism at the service of the consciousness soul.[23]

The dangerous strength of Sorath is nowhere more plainly demonstrated than by the fact that Christ Himself, in order to remove the main thrust of the attack, was obliged to advance His incarnation, which should have taken place in the middle of the fourth post-Atlantean epoch (that is, in AD 333) by 333 years. It is only Christ, as Logos-bearer, who is capable of providing the balance against Sorath, whereby his attack was largely foiled. His plan was only partially realized. Christ forestalls Sorath; but to meet him in the right, balancing way, He is in a certain sense compelled to alter the moment of His appearance on earth. Human beings take no direct part in this confrontation between spiritual beings. It would in any case have been far beyond their capability. Through the 333 years before and after the mid-point of the fourth post-Atlantean epoch, the date AD 666 as the planned entry of Sorath's activity comes about. As a result of this new discovery by Rudolf Steiner it is clear that Sorath has a direct influence on historical development. The repetition of this number of years brings an ever-strengthening intention of Sorath along with it, whereby the years 1332, 1998, 2664 and so on are to be understood as the nodal points of events which stretch over longer periods of time, as for instance throughout the whole twentieth century.

Even though Christ has counteracted the full extent of Sorath's activity there still remain significant effects upon the historical process. A few points will now be stressed because they are of immense importance for both the present and the future.

In the consciousness soul one first comes to terms as a personality with the forces of egoism. Thereby a person's spirituality is concealed from him. But his consciousness has to expand. He must consciously take hold of his 'I' as a spiritual being in the spiritual world. Rudolf Steiner expresses it as follows: 'In the age of the consciousness soul man can become man only by becoming conscious of what he is; otherwise he remains an animal, lags behind in his human evolution.'[24]

It is Sorath's intention to prevent this acquisition of an extended consciousness that raises mankind up to become man. Out of that there arises a tremendous opposition to a healthy spiritual extension of consciousness, which is everywhere apparent—a resistance towards awakening to the spirit, which has to be overcome, otherwise man will be cast down to the animal stage. First he remains stationary, then he becomes retrograde. This tendency is one of the symptoms of our time.

Another result for mankind was characterized by Rudolf Steiner a few days later in his lecture in Zürich, 'How do I find the Christ?' He there explains, among other things, how 'to put it rather trivially, the Sorath impulse, in spite of being blunted, gave mankind a slight inner "kink", which works right down into the physical body. At that time humanity was given an impulse, which is transmitted even into the physical body and which we still are born with today.'[25]

This is further characterized by Rudolf Steiner with a different turn of phrase, 'Mankind has a thorn in the flesh,' prophetically alluded to by Paul (2 Corinthians 12:2). 'But this thorn will become more and more universal, will gain more and more in importance.'[26]

This weakness, this thorn in the flesh, produces an illness

which causes people to become deniers of God if they are unable to overcome it. With that again tendencies of our time become understandable, the strength of which comes from the abyss from which they emerge.

Another characteristic of Sorath is concisely stated by Rudolf Steiner: 'But the aim of the being who hoped to intervene in 666 was to make himself God.'[27] That means, he wanted to take the place of God for mankind; he was filled with what constitutes the Antichrist. This is expressed in the self-deification tendency of some dictators of the twentieth century—a will to power which despises and destroys mankind, for Sorath is not intent on freeing man but on enslaving him.

In many of his lectures Rudolf Steiner referred from many different points of view to the Eighth Ecumenical Council of 869, in which—as he formulated it—the spirit was abolished. It is of the greatest significance that this event within the Catholic Church is here portrayed as emanating from Sorath.[28] As far as I am aware, this is only mentioned in the lecture of 11 October 1918. He says there:

> The being who hoped to intervene in 666 said: 'Men will come who no longer direct their gaze to the spirit—the spirit will not interest them. I shall see to it' (and this he actually brought about) 'that in the year 869 a Council will be held in Constantinople at which the spirit will be abolished. Men will no longer be interested in the spirit; they will turn their attention to nature and form ghostlike concepts of nature.'[29]

That shows on the one hand how an institution which calls itself Christian is able to take up an antichristian impulse and pursue it for centuries, because, undoubtedly, its origin is completely shrouded in darkness. What really counts is not the name or cause you espouse, but the realities underlying it.

On the other hand it cannot be denied that the dogma of

the duality of man in body and soul—the reality of the human spirit having been lost—has meanwhile become a generally accepted doctrine, which extends far beyond the circle of the Catholic Church. This teaching dominates psychology in an infinite number of ways, so that the soul considers itself to be something purely subjective—that is to say, a boundless subjectivism is diffused. That is the easily comprehensible result of the fact that, through the abolition or denial of the spirit, the objective and at the same time cosmic part of man is condemned to ineffectiveness. One could also say that the soul which lacks orientation through the spirit is thrown back onto the body. Through that, in continuation of the Sorath principle, the strong tendency arises for the soul also to be abolished, as was the spirit, and to be looked on as just another appendage of the body and bodily functions. The rescue of the soul demands the rediscovery of spirit reality.

The aims of Sorath were to have been realized on earth in the year 666 through the Academy of Gundeshapur. They did not achieve full success because the Mystery of Golgotha had already taken place. The teachings which were given there 'formed the greatest imaginable contrast to all that has developed from the Event of Golgotha'.[30] Rudolf Steiner speaks about the great teacher in Gundeshapur 'whose name is unknown, but who was the greatest opponent of Christ Jesus'.[31]

This brief note is important for the fact that it describes a human being who pre-eminently provides a vessel for Sorath to inhabit, although there is never a question of it being an incarnation. Rather does it suggest that the wisdom of the Beast, that is Sorath, was planned 'by certain higher spirits, particularly by a being of ahrimanic nature who was to lead these spirits, who was to appear, even if not on the physical plane'.[32]

If one takes this all together, three stages are defined: Sorath, the Beast, as the impulse-giver; an ahrimanic being as inspirer; a human being, who, so to speak, propagates and acts as the representative on earth of his doctrines. With that an indication is given of the co-operation between Sorath and the ahrimanic beings, which have several characteristics in common. Finally let me mention a very strange course of events which shows in a certain sense what difficulties there were for the Christ-impulse to counter the intentions of Sorath. For something had to be introduced that was problematical, even oppositional. 'Through the appearance of Mohammed what was to have gone out from Gundeshapur was weakened and held back.'[33] Something was thereby brought about on the historical plane which adversely affected and undermined the propagation of the teachings of Gundeshapur. As a result of that a certain relationship between the Gundeshapur teachings and Mohammedanism has come about, which is important at the present day.

Altogether, through the descriptions of the Sorath being which Rudolf Steiner gave in 1918, we can see that Sorath's influence has flowed — unconsciously and unrecognized — into western historical development in diverse ways. Thus it can be of no surprise that this impulse is very strongly felt in the twentieth century, especially because of the fact that Sorath's number is being repeated for the third time — 1998.

# 4
## *The Encounter with the Apocalyptic Beast, the Year 1933*

The description of Sorath given by Rudolf Steiner from 11 October 1918 onwards has a parallel in the change of character that took place in Adolf Hitler as a result of gas poisoning and temporary loss of sight. The remarkable fact has already been referred to[34] that in the same days that Rudolf Steiner was speaking about the historic intervention of the Sorath being, those happenings were taking place in Ypres which were a preparation for the greatest historical intervention of Sorath. Once again one's attention is drawn to the fact that the words and actions of Rudolf Steiner are guided by higher spiritual obligations in respect of time and place. In the present case it is a matter of an event which arises out of deeper historical necessity being met by a penetrative recognition which will be of importance for a growing number of people in the future. Before all else, however, it is decisive for Sorath to be met with conscious recognition on the physical plane. It has been shown time and time again that the element of recognition, especially in the case of Sorath but also in that of Ahriman, is a matter of vital importance. For in their way of working, Sorath and Ahriman are highly dependent on *not* being recognized. And it is always amazing to see how weakly developed are the powers of discernment and how little one acts on what one professes to believe in.

Thus, when Hitler—showing his true guise—openly states: 'The work begun by Christ, I will bring to a conclusion,'[35] his blasphemous presumption and megalomaniacal arrogance were discerned by few people.

But this is not to suggest that the activity of Hitler from

1933 onwards was an inevitable stroke of fate. Simply because the year 1933 is significant in the unfolding of Christianity as the time of the approaching Etheric Christ, and because corresponding counter-effects might therefore be expected, this does not mean that events *had* to happen as they did.

In order to understand this we must turn our attention to 9 November 1918. According to what Hitler wrote in *Mein Kampf*, this 9 November was the trigger that released his political career. ('But I decided to become a politician!') This was directed from the very start, and with the greatest power of will, to realizing a delusion of huge proportions. Carried by the fairy-tale of Germany's military invincibility—in grotesque contrast to the reality—revenge was to have been carried out against those who were responsible for its apparent ruin. The hate was directed against the supposed perpetrators, against Marxists and Jews. The new Germany, the Thousand-year Empire, was to have been built up on lies, revenge and hate.

In contrast to that were the efforts of Rudolf Steiner to enlighten the German people with a true insight into their situation. That was served mainly by his leaflet: 'An Appeal to the German Nation and to the Civilized World' (Spring 1919) in which he attributes the fall of the German Empire, founded in 1871, and the consequent ending of the monarchy to a 'fatal error'.

Where can the reasons for this fateful error be found? This question must now call forth a process of self-evaluation within the soul of every German. Will there be enough strength left for such introspection? Germany's very existence depends upon it. Germany's future also hinges upon the sincerity of the questioning mind—how did we fall prey to such fatal misconceptions? If reflection upon this inquiry starts immediately, then it will come in a flash of understanding: yes, we did found an empire half a century ago, but we neglected to give it a task springing from within the very essence of its national spirit.³⁶

Here appeal is made to us to develop self-knowledge, to recognize the fundamental error of not providing the Empire with 'a task springing from within the very essence of its national spirit', as the memorable formula puts it. The catastrophe which befell the German Empire was not caused by outer factors nor by the failures of incapable people, but by spiritual vacuity—the inner hollowness which did not produce either a task or a goal. In this Empire the German nation had been forsaken by its good genius; it had long since ceased to let itself be guided by its true active spirit. The spiritual void drew the demons of war and destruction irresistably towards it. It would have needed the utmost exertion of self-reflection in order to have acquired the knowledge on which depended 'the very existence of the German nation'. The horrible truth is that at that time there were far too few people who could seriously have undertaken this step in knowledge, as is evident, when we look at the present century in which the capacity to learn from catastrophes is minimal at the best of times. Even after more that 75 years there can be no question of this knowledge having been attained to a sufficient degree, though this is not any more strictly relevant. To the historical conscience, however, it remains a task that still has to be carried out.

Lack of knowledge about the real cause of the catastrophe had fatal historic consequences for the world. Only an honest and wholehearted admission of the mistakes would have made people appreciate the new insight which Rudolf Steiner later incorporated into his 'appeal'. This insight showed that the structure of the centralized state, which had developed through the centuries out of pre-Christian religious institutions, was basically no longer in a position to support human evolution in a sound and fruitful manner in the age of the consciousness soul.

Rudolf Steiner wished to provide insight into the fact that humanity stands in the social sphere before a tremendous upheaval which, in the words of Nietzsche, is a 'revaluing of all values'.

'The forces at work in modern times urge recognition of a social structure for all humanity that comprehends something entirely different from prevailing views. Heretofore, social communities have been largely shaped by human social instincts. The task of the times must be to permeate these forces with full consciousness.'[37]

Rudolf Steiner points out the error of looking upon the social organism as a unified structure. Since the time of the French Revolution with its ultimately unclear and misunderstood ideals of Freedom, Equality and Brotherhood, evolution demands that these impulses should no longer be directed towards a unity but towards a threefold social order, the sections of which are governed by different, even contradictory rules. Rudolf Steiner sums up the characteristics of these sections as follows:

> Economic life can prosper only if it develops according to its own laws and energies as an independent system within the social organism, and if it does not let confusion upset its structure by permitting another part of the social order—that which is at work in politics—to invade it. On the contrary, the political system must function independently alongside the economic system, just as in the natural organism breathing and thinking function side by side. Their wholesome collaboration can be attained only if each member has its own vitally interacting regulations and administration. However, beneficial interaction falters if both members have one and the same administrative and regulatory organ. If it is allowed to take over, the political system is bound to destroy the economy, and

the economic system loses its vitality if it becomes political.

> These two spheres of the social organism must now be joined by a third that is shaped quite independently, from within its own life-possibilities — the cultural sphere, with its own legitimate order and administration. The cultural portions of the other two spheres belong in this sphere and must be submitted to it; yet the cultural sphere has no administrative power over the other two spheres and can influence them only as the organic systems coexisting within a complete natural organism influence each other.[38]

What Rudolf Steiner deemed necessary in the situation of 1919 he formulated in such a way that it depended on circumstances and it has remained so ever since.

> Disaster ought to give rise now to introspection. The will to make the social organism possible must be developed. A new spirit — not the Germany of the past, which had created an impossible social structure out of the confusion of the three systems — should now confront the external world. A new Germany with *cultural, economic and politicial systems*, each with its own administrations, should now begin the work of rebuilding relationships with the victor.[39]

The concept of a 'possible social organism' here used by Rudolf Steiner, points to the fact that the forces of man's spiritual reality were ripe to embrace a new threefold social order. In the age of freedom, however, true spiritual possibility needs to be understood and then above all got hold of by the will. The world-historic opportunity was missed, however. Rudolf Steiner indicated very clearly the consequences that would arise — and have arisen — if the 'practical people', that is, the politically responsible ones, like all who share in the social organism, do not acquire the necessary insight.

'They will have to realize: one will either have to bring oneself to comply with the demands of reality, or one will not have learned anything from the misfortune and will have increased it by unlimited further happenings.'[40]

The terrible experience that nothing was done about it is a characteristic of the century.

Through a comprehensive view of the past it becomes clear that in a spiritual sense the Threefold Social Movement provided the *possibility* of powerfully opposing the Beast in 1933. It was—as has already been stated—no inexorable fate which was enacted, even though one is clearly aware that the fateful event was bound to come. But it is not unjustified to imagine that lesser degrees of the Beast's effect could have come about. That has nothing to do with the fact that the course of world history as it appears in retrospect has to be acknowledged to be necessary. As a result of the inability to correct, by means of the Threefold Movement after the First World War, the whole wrong development of the nineteenth century, which signified 'a loss of *identity*, a break with their folk-spirit' for the German nation, the catastrophe was increased to a hideous and unthinkable degree.[41]

How the threefold state would have fared against Hitler's machinations can easily be discerned from his radical insistence on the principle of the centralized state. This principle of the centralized state had completed its mission. It had been dead since at least 1917 and through its decease attracted the ahrimanic and sorathic forces in the most powerful manner. This is expressed in Hitler's so-called assumption of power. Hitler was absolutely fanatical about a unified state, not merely through his brutal concentration of power in his own hand in the sense of '*One* people, *one* Empire, *one* leader!' but also because his instinct for power told him that this was the only thing that could serve him as a tool. That is also confirmed by the fact that Hitler rightly regarded the Threefold Movement as his enemy from early on in his career. Thus he turned against the then German Secretary of State for Foreign Affairs, Simons (he was of Jewish descent), in a leading article in the paper *Völkische Beobachter* (People's Observer) on 15 March 1921, under the heading: 'Statesmen or National Criminals'. He called him 'an intimate friend of the gnostic and anthroposophist Rudolf Steiner, adherent of the Threefold Commonwealth, or whatever these Jewish methods for the disruption of people's normal attitude of mind might be called'.[42] If one takes into account the fact that, on principle, Hitler felt no obligation towards truth, and that he invariably turned it on its head, such a statement seems very telling, as does his desire to 'turn back the wheel of history to a time previous to 1789'. He dreamed of a time in which the unified state still had unlimited legitimacy.

The above-mentioned will-impulse of Sorath to make himself the false God of humanity, to put himself in the place of Christ, to be in fact the Antichrist, was very active in Hitler previous to 1933 and especially after that time.[43] His statement quoted above makes that clear: 'The work begun by Christ, I will bring to a conclusion!' It was and is indispensable, in view of the Hitler phenomenon, that it is seen as a spiritual event in the sense that the reality of the spiritual world and its beings — though in this case evil — is recognized and accepted. One could almost say that the phenomenon of Hitler rouses us to the greatest extent to truly take the spirit seriously. But in spite of the most far-reaching and unending research into the facts, this has still not come about, though in places it is perfectly obvious. The unsatisfactory (because indecisive) results of many accounts is caused by the fading of the spiritual dimension, which is one of the results of the 'abolition of the spirit'. Also the commonly used expression 'unredeemed past' is related, at least in part, to the fact that in general one has not on the whole succeeded in blunting Hitler's attack by recognizing that it is a *spiritual* phenomenon. For it is self-evident that Sorath—as with all evil beings—does not want to be recognized, and that a change for the better comes about when he is recognized for what he is. This change for the better, through the recognition of the reality of the spirit, has only come about to the smallest extent until now; it belongs, however, to the act of withstanding the encounter with the apocalyptic Beast.

It is wholly insufficient to describe Hitler as a medium, as a psychopath and as a criminal. All of these descriptions are certainly correct and can be confirmed in countless examples, but they tend to conceal the essential fact. Thus the dispute among historians as to whether Lenin and Stalin or Hitler were the first to perpetrate the most terrible crimes against humanity is ultimately of no account, for in both cases the catastrophe is attributed to criminal human souls and not to the impulse of wicked beings which far exceeds them.

Nevertheless, we should not fail to recognize or acknowledge that there are and were—as ever—certain individuals who tore aside the masking veil. As an ever-shining example of recognition we can name the Scholl sisters and their friends belonging to the *Weisse Rose* (White Rose) who wrote a broadsheet in autumn 1942 at the time of the siege of Stalingrad, which stated:

> Every word which issues from Hitler's mouth is a lie: when he says peace, he means war, and when he utters the name of the Almighty in the most profane manner, he means the might of the Evil One, the fallen Angel, Satan. His mouth is the stinking throat of Hell and his might is basically vile. One must surely take up the fight against the National Socialist terror-state by rational means; but whoever doubts the reality of demonic powers today has no idea of the background of this war. Behind what is

concrete and physically observable, behind all objectively logical considerations stands the irrational factor of battle against the demon, against the envoy of the Antichrist.[44]

This astonishing and admirable feat of knowledge, accomplished by the circle of the young people who arrived at this conviction out of their own experience, tore the mask from Hitler's face.

It is significant that the Führer and the Nazi leaders reacted so sensitively. They were right in feeling that their rule of power was seriously endangered by this unmasking. The Gestapo hunted feverishly for the culprits. When they were discovered by accident in February 1943, the trial was begun within a few days, as though to deal with the dangerous situation as quickly as possible. Hitler himself signed the death warrant for the young people and ordered them to be executed immediately by guillotine.

In this connection we should think again about Hermann Kükelhaus who called Hitler and his henchmen a 'cosmic carcinoma', a highly spiritual form of concept which clearly expresses its supersensible origin as well as its power to destroy all forms.[45] This form of concept can be deepened and extended.

We should not forget the work of Karl Heyer (1888–1964), who as a contemporary and a person immediately involved, followed the development of Hitler and National Socialism minutely, recording and working on it to create a unique store of information and enlightening thoughts.[46] This achievement of Heyer was possible through the intensive study of anthroposophy as also through an energetic pursuance of the path of knowledge.

In order to become better acquainted with the nature of Sorath we shall return to what the previous Secretary of State for Foreign Affairs, Joachim von Ribbentrop, wrote about the personality of the 'Führer'.

This was written by him in 1946 for his advocate in the Nuremberg war criminals trial at which, as one of those chiefly responsible, he was condemned and put to death. The incredible contrast between Hitler's appearance during the First World War up to 1918 and that of later times is illuminated by the amazing fact that in the four years of war Hitler made no name for himself. In the First World War his Commanding Officer considered making the Lance Corporal into a Non-commissioned Officer. They did not do so because 'we cannot find any of the right leadership qualities in him'.[47] To begin with we shall quote a few sentences of Ribbentrop, which characteristically enough describe Hitler's attitude to him and others.

> In 1933 I got to know Hitler better. If, however, someone were to ask me today if I knew him well, how he thought as a politician and statesman, what sort of person he was, I would have to admit that I know very little about him, actually nothing at all. The fact is that, although I have experienced so much with him, I have not got any closer to him humanly or otherwise in all our years of working together than I was on the first day we were acquainted. There was something in his whole being which was indescribably aloof.[48]

And a little later we hear:

> To judge the character of a person, a genius such as Adolf Hitler, is very difficult. One cannot measure him by ordinary standards. His most notable features were his burning patriotism and his fanatical determination to make Germany great. He was convinced of his mission for which he regarded himself as chosen by destiny. He possessed an inflexible will and an unimaginable energy in carrying out his aims. His power of comprehension and intelligence was stupendous.[49]

Ribbentrop gives an honest account of his relationship to Hitler.

'I openly admit that in the course of our working together his whole personality, his eyes and his whole manner put one under a magnetic spell ... like many others I hung on to Adolf Hitler with remarkable affection and adoration.'[50]

In this one witness a millionfold phenomenon is clearly described. One shudders at the abyss of error to which the best human forces were exposed. The tremendous force of will which it shows causes complete fascination which prevents any questions being asked about its origin. The reversal of values which is described in the broadsheet of the 'White Rose' cannot be recognized. The active will shrouds it in deepest darkness. This effect is impressively described by Ribbentrop in connection with individual personalities in what follows:

> I have seen strong personalities go to Hitler with their breast full of all the truths they want to tell him — how a catastrophe will occur if this or that is not abolished and they will not take any responsibility for the results, and so on. At the end of half an hour they come away from Adolf Hitler beaming and satisfied and arguing for the views of Hitler with just as much enthusiasm as they had when they went in, but often for views which are the exact opposite. It has often happened to me too, but perhaps with not quite the same enthusiasm as the others — but nevertheless I was convinced. I once spoke about Hitler with the politician Todt, who had known him for many years when he visited me in London. I spoke about the great influence which Adolf Hitler had on everybody, even foreigners, and also on me personally. Todt then said to me that Hitler had always possessed the power in his eyes to either eliminate, or at least paralyse the thinking capacity of others. He had known that for a long

time and this was one, albeit only *one* of the secrets of the power that Adolf Hitler had over other people.[51]

The sought for and desired control over another human being to the point of complete subjection, as described here so vividly, is an essential symptom of the working of the Antichrist. Ultimately it is a question of an assault on the ego. One should not easily believe that one could have stood up against this well-directed power of ego-elimination. Basically it has been achieved by only very few who were in direct contact with Hitler—for instance Erwin Rommel, who first admired Hitler but then, because of Hitler's military irresponsibility, was repulsed by him and rejected him. In a consultation he would not be satisfied with empty words; he stuck up against Hitler and held to his own opinion. Although Hitler had a tremendous respect for Rommel and had made him his Field Marshal, he could not stand that. After the assassination attempt on 20 July 1944, with which Rommel was only marginally connected, he had to pay the price with a brutally enforced suicide through potassium cyanide. That shows once more the complete lack of compassion, the ruthless cruelty of the will.

Essential in this connection is the statement which refers back to Todt, when he says that Hitler 'had always possessed the power in his eyes to either eliminate or at least paralyse the thinking capacity of others'. Therewith is described the most effective way of gaining entry into the will of another person. If one understands this correctly then nothing can more strongly underline the importance of the independent ego-orientated thinking than this statement. It corresponds with the above-mentioned advice of Rudolf Steiner in respect of black magicians and the triumphant words of Mephisto: 'reason and knowledge only thou despise, the highest strength in man that lies!' Wherever human thought ceases—irrespective of the cause—a gateway is opened in the soul for the influence of Sorath to enter.

Hitler's way of working was different when he was confronted with a large audience—with the 'mass', as he expressed it. Here we shall quote a description by Ribbentrop in this connection:

> The tremendous self-assurance which emanated from him and the often inconceivable severity of his will which went hand in hand with a brilliant, simple and understandable way of expressing himself, spoke to the hearts of all who had anything to do with him and forced them to come under his spell. I once stood in a great assembly of many hundreds of thousands of people and observed how the words of Adolf Hitler stirred the crowd. Enthusiasm, anger, sympathy and love of Adolf Hitler which brought them to tears was evident on every hand. I said then that the personality of this man, in the effect it had on people and on crowds, was the greatest phenomenon of all times.[52]

The effect here described is the result of Hitler's words and gestures. In Munich in 1919, Hitler had the experience 'I could speak!' with which he described the magical effect he had on his audience.[53] This effect was consciously cultivated by him and became tremendously enhanced in the course of time. The words which Hitler knew how to manipulate very skilfully would hardly have achieved this effect on their own. One can notice this if one reads the texts of his speeches today. Looking at these texts one can be astonished that they could have produced any kind of effect at all, but that is to forget that they were spoken words and, above all, accompanied by gestures.

By gestures we mean here those gestures and movements which he let the crowd make. Nothing has a greater effect on the human will than mimicked movements. To achieve the greatest unconscious effect on the will it is preferable that these are repeated as often as possible and are as little understood as possible. This formula was always used by Hitler to perfection: marching in step to the stupefaction of one's own will and the strengthening of the other's will, drilling, followed by anticipatory standing and waiting, speaking in chorus. A special role can be attributed without doubt to the Hitler salute as a combination of speech and movement; nor should we forget the above-mentioned self-idolization tendency of Sorath, for the word *heil* can really only be used in the German language with reference to God or to something divine. When he appeared in public Hitler repeated this movement countless times. The crowd mimicked this gesture and identified itself with that which issued from Hitler. Just as we can use Hitler as a foil to help recognize the true meaning of thinking, so we can also recognize the meaning of an art of movement such as Eurythmy, the aim of which is to consciously make visible, in a free and responsible manner, the unseen forces streaming through movement. What was done by Hitler in this connection was, in its way, a brilliant anti-Eurythmy, through which we are enabled to conjecture the possibilities of healing and strengthening latent in this sphere of activity.

But there is still another aspect of activity which has to be taken into account if we are to understand how Hitler managed to gain contact with so many human beings. In Guido Knopp's book *Hitler — eine Bilanz* (Hitler — an analysis), the author analyses very clearly, among other things, the methods which Hitler employed.

> In the exuberance of his eloquence Hitler often gave the impression of being carried away by it and losing control over himself. But when he then paused and brushed aside the demons of passionate emotion with an angry movement of the hand, the artificiality of the temperamental outburst remained obvious to the keen observer.

For a short while the posturer allowed one to become aware of the fact that he was quite well aware of what he was saying and of what he wished to achieve thereby. And also when he flung his tirades of hate into the auditorium, he was at the same time in control of his ebullition. What made the effects dangerous was the combination of fanaticism and reasonableness, his own special brand of intoxication and rationality.[54]

What Knopp here describes can be seen as a perfect example of what Rudolf Steiner calls the collaboration of Lucifer and Ahriman.[55] This new kind of collaboration between the luciferic and ahrimanic impulses is a symptom of the twentieth century and—as in this case—is to be understood in such a way that the alloy of contrary forces serves Sorath and opens wide the door of the soul for the instreaming antichristian impulses antagonistic to man. At any rate, when Hitler spoke to the masses, he became, as he himself admits, 'another man' by means of which he could convey this active impulse to many people.[56] Ever and again the hypnotic effect coming from Hitler is spoken about. Hypnotism, which breaks the will of the other person, stands in complete contradiction to the dignity of the free human being.

The effect that Hitler produced on his audience is not exclusively to be laid at his door. He knew furthermore how to appeal to the latent and unconscious stirrings of his participating audience. The adversarial forces suppressed from human consciousness were made use of, and the hidden inner enemies of man, which are otherwise held in check, were stirred up. Guido Knopp describes it as follows:

Nevertheless, the whole mastery of oratorical technique and staging should not blind one to the fact that all Hitler's agitation could only flourish on the basis of a thorough agreement with his public. He uttered quite openly what his audience was privately thinking and he knew it only too well, because he came from the same world of experience. He formulated to its conclusion what people only muttered behind their hands. Hitler did not have to pursuade his followers, for at heart they were all of the same mind, at least in as far as the direction was concerned, not necessarily about the ultimate goal. The incendiary addressed himself to 'worthy gentlemen'. His words were the elegant expression of their minds.[57]

One could also say — to get nearer to the point — that the will was first approached by Sorath, whereby it depended on how far the Sorath element was already present in it. As a result of the oration this will was roused and strengthened until it finally allowed itself to be willingly accepted into the work of destruction. In this way it becomes understandable how so many people with paralysed consciences and blunted consciousness made themselves into tools, into accessories, even to accomplices and perpetrators.

It is not just to excuse themselves when such people — as though awakening from a dream — later look upon themselves, their behaviour, their deeds, as something quite foreign to their nature. That does not excuse anyone from personal responsibility for his deeds, but a spiritual-scientific perspective on the human being makes the process more understandable.

As man is always able to experience the spiritual world and the beings that dwell therein in the unconscious depths of his will, this spiritual realm is basic to what is religious, sacral, cultic. Therefore it is understandable that a movement such as Hitler's, which is so intensely directed towards the will, addresses itself to that realm and uses it for its own purposes. Enough was done in this direction, especially through mass events. Guido Knopp gives a vivid description of the mood during the election campaign of 1932 in which an aeroplane was used.

Hitler's Ascension [*Himmelfahrt* in German, which means 'heavenly journey'] over Germany not only burst the bounds of previous audience accessibility, but lent him an aura of modernity and mysticism. When the illuminated plane descended through the night sky to the waiting folk below, the message of a miraculous healer took visible shape. Flag parades, march music, the play of lights and symbolism, festive expectation and many-voiced calls of *Heil!* all contributed to increase the liturgical experience. Every bit of the show, from the planning of the route to the course of the evening, was, as Goebbels wrote, 'organized to the last detail' and everything was aimed at increasing the suggestive power of Hitler's presence. Hundreds of thousands felt his speeches as a collective emotional experience which put them into a frenzy of new horizons, satisfaction and fellow-feeling. They willingly cast aside for a few hours their healthy common sense.[58]

Once again pseudo-religious and pseudo-sacred manipulation succeeded in depriving people of their 'healthy common sense'. Moreover it was a common result of Hitler's appearance on the scene that he aroused messianic feelings — was even taken to be the Messiah — for which there is a frightening number of examples.

The overall appearance presented by Hitler makes one see that a human body and soul can serve in a unique way to become the vessel for the Sorath being. Just in order to make it clear, it must be said that we are not dealing here with an incarnation, but with a powerful possession. After the change or switch-over in October/November 1918 the possibility was always present for the alien being to enter in to replace or suffuse the ego-organization. This shows that there are degrees of the greatest penetration by another being, as also phases of almost complete desertion. Hitler's charisma, which has been described by innumerable witnesses time after time, is the eloquent expression of this state of affairs. A person whose most striking characteristic had previously been his unobtrusiveness, now suddenly assumes a quite different appearance.

In all this Sorath shows up as the being which tries with all its might to seize hold of and occupy the human will, robbing it and depriving it of freedom, because the ego, which forms concepts and is itself conceived, is not present in this realm, but exists actually—though quite unconsciously—in the reality of the spiritual world and in those beings which inhabit it. Sorath is concerned pre-eminently with the ego in the will, whereas Ahriman's point of attack is the intellect, the understanding, the life of ideation. One now finds that the two beings help one another, that they pull together, as it were, on the same strand, whereby actually the two impulses merge in practice. But in the last analysis they are quite different.

In order to highlight the difference between Christ and the Antichrist, Sorath, one can apply the word of Christ: 'I am the Way, the Truth and the Life!' to the thinking, feeling and willing, first of a person who endeavours to take the Christ-impulse into himself, and second of someone like Hitler, who is more or less filled with the power of Sorath. The former will strive to take up into his thinking the spiritual contents of anthroposophy and to overcome the many illusions which hinder him from living according to the truth. He will seek to understand the Christ-impulse. Through his feelings he will follow the path that leads from the experience of his own being to the sensing of the Christ living in the surroundings; he will come through his destiny to the experience of the second man within man, to the receiving of selfhood from without. In his will, which extends unconsciously over the threshold of the spiritual world, he will find Life, will find Existence, and will learn to know that the world of spirit which supports and helps mankind is a threefold, trinitarian, world and that this Trinity bears his ego in a manner worthy of mankind.

In the Hitler sheaths the antichristian antithesis of this appears. In his thinking the lie becomes a consciously applied tool. He himself understood propaganda to mean that it had to ruthlessly serve the hidden goal without any responsibility towards truth. The ends justified the means. Intelligence was used in an ahrimanic sense to prepare and carry out evil deeds. In the feelings only the connection to the self was realized, selfishness of emotional sensitivity which made it impossible to experience another being, to feel compassion. The will, however, is unable to free itself from the darkness of matter; it clings, as it were, to the Old Adam which, in contrast to the truth of the Trinity, holds inflexibly to the principle of oneness. Thus arises the unhappy connection to 'blood and territory' which proves so disastrous, because the blood which is referred to here has long since become decadent and the territory, or the earth, conceals subterranean powers which would drag down and destroy mankind.

We shall try in another way to make clear the aforementioned contrast in its full dimension. It was described how Sorath addresses the human will directly, lays hold of and makes use of it through the way in which his strange servant Hitler was able to work on people. By that means the active 'I' was stunned and came close, through assimilation into the 'masses', to which Hitler so liked to refer, to becoming extinguished. From that point, from the lower will-forces, it worked itself upwards into feelings and thinking in such a way that the heart became sluggish, compassion died, conscience fell asleep and thinking lost its connection with reality. It is a current in man which streams from below upwards.

The movement beneficial to man is the exact opposite of this. It starts out from the 'I' which lives in the consciousness pole, in order that freedom may be properly acknowledged. Only the 'I' itself may approach the spirit of its own accord and to this it is led by destiny. For only out of this individually determined precondition is the 'I' able to absorb spiritual contents in a fruitful way, become acquainted with them and work on them. Thus one can eventually gain independent understanding and free insight. For that reason the anthroposophical method describes supersensible contents and provides facts with which the conscious 'I' can freely deal. A direct influence on feelings and will must never be exerted. The way to these can be found by the 'I' of its own accord if it acquires spirituality; for certainly feelings and will have to be transformed, but only by way of the conscious 'I'. That is the Michaelic way of the consciousness soul, which seeks the Christ Spirit in feeling and willing along the path of conscious spiritualized thinking.

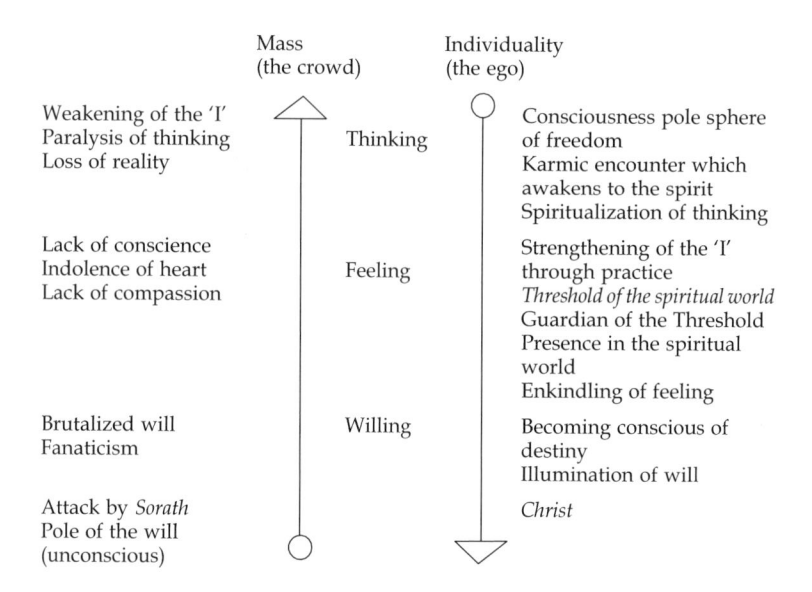

|  | Mass (the crowd) | Individuality (the ego) |
|---|---|---|
| Weakening of the 'I' Paralysis of thinking Loss of reality | Thinking | Consciousness pole sphere of freedom Karmic encounter which awakens to the spirit Spiritualization of thinking |
| Lack of conscience Indolence of heart Lack of compassion | Feeling | Strengthening of the 'I' through practice *Threshold of the spiritual world* Guardian of the Threshold Presence in the spiritual world Enkindling of feeling |
| Brutalized will Fanaticism | Willing | Becoming conscious of destiny Illumination of will |
| Attack by *Sorath* Pole of the will (unconscious) |  | *Christ* |

Rudolf Steiner made statements about these two contrasting paths, which can help us to deepen our knowledge in this respect very considerably. In his lecture cycle *From Jesus to Christ*, Rudolf Steiner calls the subconscious soul-life (which remains unrecognized in its content, though not unrecognizable in principle) the 'Son' or 'Logos', in contradistinction to the conscious soul-life that is known as the 'spirit'. The third principle of the Trinity, the 'Father', is in this connection 'nature', as it works as the element of existence in the world and man. The task now remains 'to prize and esteem the realm of the Son or Logos, to prize and esteem the domain of the subconscious ... as an inviolable sanctuary that should rest in the personality, in the individuality of each human being, a sanctuary which should only be approached through the door of conscious knowledge. This, at least, is how a modern consciousness should approach it, i.e. a consciousness that belongs to our age.[59]

The relationship that a person has to Christ in the depths of his still unconscious being is only able to develop if it can, unhindered and undisturbed, follow the laws integral to it. That is made plain by the following words of Rudolf Steiner:

> Those who have taken to themselves the name of 'Rosicrucian' have desired to preserve this impulse of Christian evolution most carefully, as far as human weakness permits. They have at all times wished to adhere most carefully to the rule that even in the highest regions of initiation nothing else must be worked upon than that which, as common between man and man, is at our disposal in the evolution of humanity, that it is only in the spirit-domain that man may work. The initiation of the Rosicrucians was an initiation of *spirit*. It was never an initiation of the will, for the will of man was something to be respected as a sanctuary in the innermost part of the

soul. For this reason the individual was led to those initiations which were to take him beyond the stage of Imagination, Inspiration and Intuition, but only so far that he could recognize within himself that which was to be evoked through the development of the spirit element. No influence was to be exercised upon the element of the will. We must not mistake this attitude for one of indifference in regard to the will. The point is that by the exclusion of direct influence upon the will, the purest spiritual working was allowed for in a mediated way through the spirit. When we come to an understanding with another human being about entering on the path of knowledge of the spirit, light and warmth are sent up from the spiritual path, and these then enkindle the will, but always by the indirect path through the spirit—never otherwise. Consequently in Rosicrucianism, in the highest sense, that impulse of Christianity is observed which finds twofold expression: on the one side in the Son-element, in the Christ-working which goes down deeply into subconsciousness; on the other, in spirit-working which embraces all that falls within the horizon of our consciousness. We must indeed bear the Christ in our will, but the way people should come to an understanding with each other about the Christ can only lie, according to Rosicrucianism, in penetrating deeper and deeper into the occult nature of conscious soul-life.[60]

Rudolf Steiner connects the opposite path to Jesuitism.

The radical, the fundamental difference between what we justifiably call the Christian way of the spirit and the Jesuit way of the spirit, which gives a one-sided exaggeration to the Jesus-principle, is that the intention of the Jesuit-way is to work at all times *directly* upon the will, at all times directly, immediately to lay hold of the will.[61]

The Jesuit training, which we shall not discuss here, has the aim of giving the greatest possible strength to the will. To characterize it we must ask what aspect of the soul-life has been directly attacked. The element that ought to be considered as immediately holy, that which ought not to be touched—the will-element! In so far as in this Jesuit training the will-element has been laid hold of, because the Jesus-idea seizes the will-element completely, just so far is the concept of the dominion of Jesus exaggerated in the most dangerous way—dangerous because, through this concept, the will becomes so strong that it can work directly upon the will of another. For where the will becomes so strong through imaginations, that is to say, through occult means, it acquires the capacity for working directly upon the will of another, and hence also along all the other occult paths to which such a will can have recourse.[62]

Two things must still be mentioned in this respect. One of these was already pointed out in the book *Ere the Century Closes*, namely, that the atomic bomb and atomic energy are, in a certain sense, the legacy which Hitler left to mankind.[63]

This study of the meeting with the apocalyptic Beast cannot end without a reference to what amounts to the climax of the monstrous activities carried out in the service of Sorath. This is done in spite of some reservations, as it is such an open question. Nevertheless, it seems right to face up to the ultimate facts consciously and courageously, because only by that means can forces of opposition unfold their activity which will lead in future along the path of healing.

What is referred to here is the fact that not only were there death-factories, the technically organized mass slaughter of human beings, but the death of these people was brought about by the use of potassium cyanide. In a lecture to workmen at the Goetheanum on 10 October 1923, which of course must be read in its entirety, Rudolf Steiner made grave statements about death caused by cyanide.

But now, as we are on earth today, if we introduce potassium cyanide into our body we destroy all our movements and life forces. And the bad thing is that there is always the danger that, by so poisoning ourselves, potassium cyanide will take the soul with it and then, instead of continuing to live in the soul, we will be diffused throughout the whole world, particularly in the sunlight.

If anthroposophical knowledge could be more widely known, no one would poison himself with potassium cyanide. One would not dream of it! It is only through a materialistic view of life that people poison themselves with potassium cyanide, because they think 'dead is dead', quite irrespective of whether one dies of cyanide poisoning or by an inner process of dissipation. But that is not a matter of indifference! If one dies through inner dispersion then the soul and spirit pass into the spiritual world in the usual way; they continue to live on. But when one is poisoned by cyanide one's soul tends to accompany each little piece of one's body, namely, to expand with the nitrogen and to dissolve into the cosmos. That is the true death of soul and spirit. If people would only know that soul and spirit are the real human being, they would say: It is quite impossible that we should cause the terrible explosion which, in a delicate way has its repercussion throughout the whole of the cosmos, when somebody poisons himself with cyanide. For every person who poisons himself with potassium cyanide joins himself in a wrong way to the current which flows from the earth to the sun. And it should be possible, if one had the right instruments, to see a small explosion in the sun every time that a person poisons himself with cyanide. And the sun deteriorates through that. A human being spoils the cosmos and also the force which comes from the sun to the earth if he poisons himself with cyanide. If a person poisons himself with cyanide then it is true that he actually ruins the sun! And that is the case with every cyanide poisoning.[64]

One should remember that the perpetrators (Hitler, Goebbels, Himmler, Goering and others), as well as the millions of their victims, died by this method. That must be seen as the most terrible attack of the Sun Demon against humanity. When considering the incalculable consequences which will result, according to Rudolf Steiner, we should be careful to do no more than pose questions. Does the ruination of the sun oppose the etherization through Christ? How does death by cyanide affect the victims? How can one work in a spiritually realistic way to help to heal these human beings? Should one not feel the greatest compassion for the perpetrators of these deeds? How can both perpetrators and victims alike find the way to the next incarnation they are looking for?

These questions are directed to the serious spiritual research of the present and future. The answers can, however, only be found if people prepare themselves to take them up in an adequate, that is, a worthy, serious and responsible fashion.

# 5
# Sorath Raises his Head at the End of the Century

## His changed method of working since 1933

The influence of Sorath continues, as we can see, throughout the centuries. Without a doubt it is increasing in intensity in the twentieth century, at the end of which time Sorath's number will have reappeared for the third time in history. This colours our time with an atmosphere of antagonism towards man and Christ. The confrontation with Sorath in 1933 and beyond is to be understood as a preparation for that which now faces mankind as a test. That might be doubted on the grounds that the happenings which have already taken place appear to be unsurpassable. One can be easily assured, however, that the present situation is far more dangerous, if only for the reason that people imagine that it is less dangerous.

In the thirties and later a tremendous pressure was exerted which turned more and more into a kind of pain which led ultimately to a certain awakening of consciousness. Hitler, for instance, became noticeably less credible, his influence on his supporters ever more frightening but otherwise not so strong. Opposition against the pressure grew, of course, as demonstrated by the German Resistance Movement in which many of the participants first woke up as a result of this pressure—as for instance the (would-be) assassin Staufenberg, or the already mentioned Scholl sisters and their friends. At present, however, the situation is the reverse. One is exposed to an inner undertow, which is so insidious because it gradually creeps up on the soul unawares in tiny steps, in such a way that truth and the reality of the spiritual world become ever more shrouded in oblivion. Truly, it is so difficult to tackle such an elusive foe because he does everything to remain unnoticed. He presents an extreme challenge to the forces of consciousness.

Ever and again the powerful tendency is seen which allows the awareness of spiritual consciousness to ebb away. In its positive aspect it means that spiritual consciousness has to be engendered afresh at every moment, which demands an exceptional presence of mind and soul-power.

The dangerous situation can also be explained through the grand spiritual concept coined by Hermann Kükelhaus of the 'cosmic carcinoma'. The 'cosmic carcinoma' was and had to be overcome physically as by a surgical operation. The necessity of this proceeding is incontestable; the Hitler regime had to be abolished, its time was up. Just as an operation carried out by a surgeon to remove a carcinoma does not remove the tendency of the organism towards cancer, so is it with the 'cosmic cancer'. Quite rightly one fears the metastasis developing after an operation, for what was at first a localized process begins to become more generalized and to more or less attack the whole organism.[65]

Something similar happened with the 'cosmic carcinoma'; it metastasized. What was at that time a localized event became surreptitiously generalized later. Through that it has on the one hand become harder to see it for what it is; on the other it is, as it were, generally accepted because the consciousness of its origin and connection has been lost.

Only to mention a few examples, to which everyone can add others: in how many places in the world does one refer without embarrassment to the principle of 'blood and soil'? Also the most extreme nationalism can—as in Hitler—take its cue from the principle of the 'self-determination of nations', as advocated by Wilson, by which every crime committed by the state can be excused outwardly as being a matter of its own private concern. The military principle as an expression of the power of defence of the unified state is recognized throughout the world as something self-evident. Competitive sport in connection with nationalism is of undisputed political significance. In the case of the Olympic Games these two are combined with commerce to make it a worldwide fascination for the masses through television. Who would not admit that many of the methods of propaganda used by Hitler at the 1936 Olympiad were not perfectly applied? The unified state—in democracies in a weakened form—is a factor which actually is unquestioned. In the Islamic Fundamentalist Movement, which issued essentially from Khomeini, the unified state appeared in its most radical form as the absolute union of faith and state, the divine state. In the sense of this divinely understood truth all worldly states must be considered as the work of the devil which have to be fanatically opposed by all means available, as for instance by the religiously motivated suicide squads of the Hamas. The dangers lurking therein are underestimated in spite of warnings from many experts. And so on.

Common to all these things, with the exception of the last-named, is that they are looked upon as being sound, not sick. They are not seen as metastasis. The worst illness is the one which goes unrecognized and which therefore cannot be treated. The path of healing is only to be achieved by means of a hard-won recognition of the true state of affairs. The powers of healing for this extremely dangerous metastasis can only be looked for in the rejected, submerged and uncomprehended concept of the threefold social organism.

## The War of All against All

A further point that shows the difficulty of the situation consists in the fact that to the war existing between groups (which exists, of course, as ever) the War of All against All has been added. If one considers the War of All against All which, as it is described above, was prophesied by Rudolf

Steiner in his 'Apocalypse' cycle of lectures of 1908 as happening at the end of the whole post-Atlantean epoch, one can then regard the present crisis as the 'Little War', which springs from the same causes and represents a kind of prelude to the coming 'Big War'. For this War of All against All is the result of the 'kink' left behind in the physical body as the remains of Sorath's activity, the 'thorn' that can really lead to an incitement of the body-bound instinctive forces of egoism, which are so powerful because they are rooted undetected in the unconscious will of man. This process is brought about by materialism in the conscious thinking, which produces a 'spiritualist' as an opposite power in the will, seized hold of by ahrimanic powers to produce 'the highest degree of egoism in the instincts'. It brings about a 'development of the instincts, whereby one is wholly occupied with attending to bodily needs and not directed towards social impulses, social sympathies and the like. What is individual develops to become the egoism of the instincts.'[66]

If this cannot be countered by the development of spiritual consciousness, we will then be left 'at the end of the twentieth century with the War of All against All, in those very parts of the world in which the so-called new culture has evolved'.[67]

After having first explained the War of All against All as processes within the human being, Rudolf Steiner then goes on to describe how this works out in the social sphere.

> Whoever observes, with a bleeding heart, how in the materialists of the nineteenth century (that is the majority of people) the opponent is lurking, knows too what a great need there is for this 'spiritualist' to rise up out of the unconscious into the conscious. Such a person will not stir up the instincts in his ahrimanic nature; he will actually be able to create a social structure of possibility in humanity

on earth. In other words: if things are allowed to run their own course, as I have described it, under the influence which, understandably enough, results from the ideology of the nineteenth century working into the twentieth, then at the end of the twentieth century we shall be faced with the War of All against All! People can give all sorts of wonderful speeches, all kinds of scientific progress can be made, but we would still be faced with the War of All against All. We would see a humanity growing up which no longer possessed any social instinct, but would speak all the more about social affairs.[68]

What would bring about the rise of this 'spiritualist' within the human being 'from the subconscious into consciousness'? It is only through acceptance of spiritual scientific ideas, which include the reality of what is subconscious, that it would be possible to educate and arouse humanity to make at least the preliminary steps so necessary for the social organism, from unconsciousness to what is conscious. At the end of this century, to which Rudolf Steiner prophetically points, let us each ask ourselves to what extent one or other of these possible paths has become reality.

One can also recognize the War of All against All in a slightly altered form in the tendency to split up and divide, in the tensions, squabbles and intolerances which quite insurmountably take place all the time in smaller or larger communities, Of course, in the age of the consciousness soul the personality has to come first. But the best and the worst are very close together and it is often difficult to tell them apart. A strong destructive force intervenes between people, affecting even their karmic connections. Ever and again we must ask how we can find within us the forces which will enable the ideals of peace, communication and harmonious relationship to be maintained. Friendliness and friendship have become very rare.

## What must be achieved by the year 2000?

The comprehensive importance that the question of consciousness has for the end of the century and the Christ Event is shown by the explanation given by Rudolf Steiner in his lecture *The Work of the Angels in Man's Astral Body*. From the whole of this lecture, to which our attention must again be expressly drawn, only the relevant material will here be cited.

Under the direction of the Spirits of Form, the Angels create pictures in the human astral body which are at first concealed from the latter. These pictures are soul-impulses which are there to lead mankind to an elementary grasp of the other person's spirituality; through the Christ-impulse they lead to a freeing of religion from the various confessions and to an irrefutable 'insight into the spiritual nature of the world'.[69] These pictures slumbering in the astral body for the creation of the social structure of the present and the future have to be awakened through a study of spiritual science. They must become conscious in order to intervene in a healthy and fruitful way in evolution. The positive aspect of our present time is that everything is left to man's free will; that is to say, a possibility is there, a need is present, which can be grasped — or perhaps not. An exact date for this is given by Rudolf Steiner — a most rare occurrence in his whole work. It will take place already *before* the beginning of the third millennium. In no other place (if one disregards the reference to the 3 × 666 years) is there mention in such a precise way of a particular moment for the attainment of a concrete goal. And the consequences of not attaining that goal are described.

> And what would happen if earthly humanity would continue to let the most important spiritual revelation of the future go by without noticing it? If, for instance, mankind would miss the middle part (the part connected

with religious freedom), if people would fail to notice the recurrence of the Mystery of Golgotha on the etheric plane, of which I have often spoken, if they would fail to notice the reappearance of the Etheric Christ, or the other things, then what the Angels attempt to achieve by means of pictures in the astral body they would have to try to attain by other means. And what mankind does not achieve in the astral body in wakefulness would be attempted in this case by the Angels fulfilling their intentions through sleeping human beings. That is to say, what humankind would fail to notice in the waking state, causing the Angels also to miss their objective, that would have to be accomplished with the help of human physical and etheric bodies lying in bed asleep. That is where the forces would be sought for the achievement of their aims. What could not be accomplished in waking man when the awakened souls reside in the etheric and physical bodies would be brought about in the sleeping etheric and physical bodies while the human beings, who ought to be awake, are outside with their egos and astral bodies. That is the great danger for the Era of the Consciousness Soul. That is the occurrence which could still come about if mankind does not wish to turn to spiritual life before the beginning of the third millennium. It is now only a short time until the beginning of the third millennium. The third millennium starts, as you know, with the year 2000. It could still happen that what has to be achieved for the work of the Angels with waking mankind will have to be achieved with the sleeping bodies of man. It may be that the Angels will have to withdraw the whole of their work from the human astral bodies in order to sink it into the etheric bodies to achieve their ends. But humanity would not be present in it![70]

From this description the decision-making character of the end of the century is strongly emphasized. It is only by being awake that the best of the forces which the Hierarchies have implanted into the astral bodies can be preserved from being changed into the worst forces, for the Hierarchies have set their faith in the awakening of the ego and they cannot withdraw their impulses again. Catastrophes, which Rudolf Steiner further describes, will of necessity occur if what is foreseen is not taken up. The reappearance of the Etheric Christ is an experience of waking up, at first for those who experience it themselves but later on, through its very presence, for all other people. It will become a transforming process for the environment.

The time organism also has to be taken into account at the end of the century — which, since the life of Jesus Christ, has had the 33-year intervals impressed into it.[71] Apart from the relationship 1965-98, which is not under consideration here, two other points must receive attention.[72]

With the end of the century a hundred years will have elapsed since the beginning of the Age of Light. Largely unnoticed, but still guarded in the soul experiences of individuals who searched for and found the new Light, this spiritual Light of Christ has received an ever-increasing illuminating power that contrasts strongly with the growing darkness. Light and darkness confront each other like Ahura-Mazda and Ahriman at the time of Zarathustra; but now so transformed by the Mystery of Golgotha that the Light has become a mild, penetrating one which shines through the darkness from below, whereas the darkness has become more intense through having rejected the Light.

On the other hand we should remember that the years 1930-33 have now passed for the second time through the 33-year cycle, or are about to do so, and through that have gained still greater significance. The circles that spread out from an event that has entered into the stream of history become ever larger until they finally ebb away. This enlargement of the circles denotes at the same time that they become more subtle, whereby the above described tendency towards a hidden, not easily discernible effect is strengthened.[73]

## How is Sorath's activity revealed?

In order to make the activity of Sorath thoroughly conscious to man we must focus clearly on his aims and ambitions. How these are expressed in individuals and what Sorath can ultimately achieve or fail to achieve is another question and one which everyone must decide for himself.

As the Sun Demon, or Antichrist, Sorath's primary aim is to destroy the work of Christ, to extirpate what Christ has done for mankind. This applies in the first place to the fundamental fact of Christianity, to the Resurrection and restoration of the spiritual-physical 'phantom' or resurrection body, which is to become the appropriate vessel for the human 'I'.[74] Furthermore, however, it is connected with the fact that the Christ-impulse seeks to awaken the spirituality of every human 'I', whereby this 'I' begins a process of development that will make it into a 'citizen of both worlds'. When the 'I' — in the sense of St Paul — takes up Christ into itself, it connects with the source of development and tranformation that will lead man's whole being to spirituality in Manas, Buddhi and Atman. Sorath is now the direct enemy of all development; he wants to block up this source of evolution, he desires stagnation. If he should succeed in this through his mighty will, it would be a triumph for him.

Specifically applied to the human being, his intention is to do away with the 'I' altogether, or at least to try to prevent it taking up the Christ-impulse. If he were to succeed in this the 'I' would remain behind in its personal development.

Sorath wants to bring about a state within the thinking, feeling and willing of man that will promote his own intentions. This touches upon salient symptoms of our time. The thinking is to remain attached to the physical-material brain, so that, acting as a mirror, it will provide man with a mere reflection of the world, a concept without any reality. Everything is done to keep the thinking so lifeless that it is paralysed, for by being active it could be launched on the path that brings about revival. The passivity of intellectual thinking makes the soul into an observer of the world, and the lack of connection with reality is thereby so strengthened that the sense activities, too, are interpreted as not connecting mankind to real world values.

In order to understand the way these impulses work we should be reminded of the fact that the sense activities bring people into a complex intentional connection to their own bodies and to the surrounding world. This opens up the possibility for the 'I' to enter the spiritual world by way of the senses, because the qualities observed by the senses are rooted in the spiritual world.[75] 'The way to the spirit is revealed to man through the senses,' as Schiller so beautifully expresses it.

The result of Sorath's activity in respect of the thinking and sense-impressions is that man should eventually lose his confidence in both; he is to be cut off from the world in which he grew up. He is led to believe that he is inescapably confined within a world of illusion. By means of technology a world is engineered by the various media which conforms to this idea.

In respect to the feelings, Sorath has the intention of binding these to the bodily nature in order to work counter to the power that leads man to develop alertness and interest in his surroundings. The aim of Sorath is easily understood if one remembers that man also connects himself with his surroundings on a feeling level during sleep and that Christ is living in these surroundings. The body-bound feeling leads to emotional irritability, to psychic self-absorption and to an exaggeration of the soul element. The excessive subjectivism that one often comes across in daily life has its place here.

While Sorath is intent on driving the individual 'I' out of the will, he intrudes into the realm in which man—deeply unconscious—seeks his karmic aims. Man has been brought into existence, with the help of all the Hierarchies, upon karmic paths through which the course of our lives is determined. This intervention in the will would render karmic causes ineffectual, would leave karma unfulfilled and the karmic intention frustrated. The 'I' is intended to develop through its karma in the sense of real progress and healing, which will live therein through the higher Hierarchies. Sorath battles in the will against the Gods of human destiny. Above all, he wants the karmic impulses, which rise up into the consciousness and seek recognition in this Age of the Consciousness Soul, to remain in the condition of sleep. Thus Sorath is the sleep-inducer in the will as against the striving for awareness of the karmic impulse.

Sorath drives the man of action into senseless acts by encouraging him to carry out actions that only serve the physical material body and do not serve other people or follow supersensible, cosmic impulses such as in Eurythmy.[76] It is he, too, who harnesses the human will to the terrible swing between paralysis and aggression.

In the human being as a whole, Sorath wants to make 'Old Adam' into his vessel, to create a reality in man that is a lie in comparison with the resurrection body. Thus the inner being of man is a stage upon which the battle against the deeds of Christ is played out; and what takes place outwardly in human wars is only a projection of this battle which Sorath wages against mankind. Just as the 'I' of man has the possibility of drawing the restored 'phantom' to itself by accepting the Christ-impulse, so does Sorath bind the 'Old Adam' to ego-centredness in order to gain the possibility of destroying the 'I'.

This aim is also served by the doctrine of the Council of 869 which was inspired by Sorath. This doctrine of the duality of body and soul is intended to become reality. Through the denial of the spirit a spiritual soul-awakening is made impossible. This is how Sorath submerges the souls into a continual soul-sleep, which is to become ever deeper, so that the 'I' (which wants to wake up) is brought into permanent oblivion. Thus it comes to what Rudolf Steiner expressed in the following way: 'Mankind is unconscious of the inner nature of God!'[77] This forgetfulness refers to the karma which is interwoven with the Hierarchies and especially with the spiritual influences borne by man out of his former lives on earth and which are so terribly difficult to get hold of consciously.

The 'soul-sleep', which is a chief characteristic of the end of the century, is the result of the direct attack of Sorath on the will, which is the most sacred part of man, for through this attack the dullness of the will is considerably increased. By means of this soul-sleep man is to be prevented from asking the real questions pertaining to the riddles of life, for, as Parsival showed us, in asking questions the 'I' awakens in the consciousness soul.

It is almost superfluous to add that Sorath is the enemy of human freedom, for that already implies a conscious achievement of the 'I'. If the abolition of the spirit was a blow to the future development of independence, Sorath intends—in close co-operation with the Asuras—to carry on the work he began by enslaving the soul to an ever greater extent to the body, so that a development towards freedom becomes impossible. On the basis of what he has already achieved, a reality is to be created which will completely exclude freedom. Sorath's power to turn his doctrines into reality is very great.

Regarding the structure of the state, it should be truthfully and radically acknowledged that at the end of the century the centralized state has won precedence; it has become the general, worldwide accepted form of human society, whether it be a dictatorship or a democracy (the structural difference between these is not as great as we are led to believe). But, in the sense of the above arguments, the worst is this: the centralized state as such is never questioned. If suggestions for reform are ever made, they do not call into question the basic principle. We have arrived at a state of complete soul-sleep of all participants in regard to the form which the social organism needs to adopt. In the realm of politics the true words of Mephisto are applicable: 'The people never scent Old Nick, e'en though he has them by the neck.' (Goethe: *Faust*, Part I, Auerbach's Cellar).

The world as we can now observe it is actually crying out for the threefold social organism. What is necessary above all else is, at the same time, completely dismissed. It is absurd to draw attention to what is needed. One is only considered to be ignorant of human realities and relationships. Certainly these are as they are, that is not to be denied. Yet it does not answer the question as to what really lies at the bottom of it all. The question regarding spiritual reality is stifled.

It is a hardly conceivable fact that millions of deaths and millionfold, immeasurable suffering has not yet led to any fundamental doubt about the centralized structure of the state. It is not only the politicians who are to blame for that, although we should not fail to see that power is sought for and clung to with the greatest intensity. It is generally accepted as a distinction if a leading politician possesses an instinct for power with which to achieve his goals.

In the sense of what has been said above about the activity of Sorath in the human being, it is evident that the structure and condition of the state and what takes place in man, unnoticed and unknown to him, are mutually reinforcing and conditional upon one another. In this respect a circuit is formed which can only be broken if — in spite of everything — more and more people become alert to the reality. As the old saying tells us: 'People get the government they deserve'.

The prevalent centralized state of today is more accurately described as a double-entity of state and economy under the tacit agreement that the spiritual life remains ineffectual, superfluous, dead. It is easy to misunderstand what is being advocated in its place — which is for spiritual reality to work directly onto the social organism in a productive way, through perceptive and creative people. (We will look at this in more detail later.) The generally deprecated collapse and loss of values makes it evident that spiritual life is not productive in this sense. Inherited values are the remains of what was formerly an effective spiritual, cultural and religious life. Their time has now passed away, they are dead. The death of the spiritual life as a renewing, creative part of the social organism has nothing to do with the artistic ability, inventiveness and store of ideas of particular individuals. Present-day cultural life has to a high degree the character of 'icing on the cake'; it is an appendix, not an essential part of the social organism that is indispensable to the health of the organism.

In the double-entity of today's state the impulses of government and economy are so intertwined that it is impossible to separate them. No serious efforts are applied to making qualitative distinctions between a government which ought to follow the principle of equality and an economy which should be predisposed towards co-operation (brotherhood). The politicians try to win votes by means of economic success, the industrialists want to increase their profits by laws favourable to their business or even by subsidies. One is constantly hearing about free enterprise or market economy, whereas everyone knows that the national states, as also the supra-state organizations, intervene in the business cycle with huge subsidies.

Self-devised principles are carried out in a grotesque manner and lead to absurdities. A significant characteristic is that people fail to take themselves seriously. It is everywhere apparent that the intellectual consciousness is losing its grasp of reality.

In the place of the spiritual life which, as above characterized, is not experienced and to the non-existence of which one has become completely accustomed, many substitutes are presented because the unsatisfied soul-life urgently demands them. What the spiritual life should accomplish is pushed down into what is private and personal and of little greater significance. The substitute for what remains unfulfilled is sought in sport, holidays, time off, things which, so to say, are outside of or on the fringe of the real current of life.

Above all, the fast-developing information and communications industry, via audio-visual media, plays an ever-increasing role. The intellectual consciousness, which reproduces the real world only as concepts via the head organization, has, with the help of technology, created a world of illusion that corresponds to it. A conceptual world is becoming ever more firmly established, is striving to create a new virtual reality in cyberspace which, however, only perfects a falsified reality.

Freedom, to which one attaches so much importance, is often nothing more than a fool's licence, a freedom for what is unimportant. It blinds one to the ineffectuality of the social organism.

With all this the human will, which is unable to work actively in the spiritual part of the social organism (to which it corresponds) because it is paralysed, remains so unfulfilled, so disengaged that a tremendous urge for experience overwhelms the soul, which then seeks by all means at its disposal to satisfy this hunger. This takes place on the one hand through aggression, conflict, violence; on the other hand through seeking what it has not experienced in a spiritual way through material means—that is, through drugs of all descriptions. By all the tragedy this entails it is easy to understand from a spiritual-scientific point of view that the will, when not engaged in what is spiritual, sinks down into the metabolic processes and seeks a safety valve there.

In present-day society other forces have developed which make it exceptionally difficult for a free spiritual life to unfold. One could have learnt from Lessing that it is not possessions but the search for truth which gives humanity its value. That does not mean, however, that there is no truth, but rather that there is no ultimate, invariable truth and that truth has to be applied tolerantly and not fanatically. Lessing strenuously defended the truths he himself had discovered. His doctrine is not intended for philistines or Pharisees to utter. A spiritual catastrophe threatens in this realm, for pluralism, relativism and subjectivism lead to a gradual dissolution of the concept of truth. One believes that one is being tolerant, but perverts the idea of truth if one is ready to accede truth to everyone. This is a false kind of tolerance that betrays lack of true discrimination. In western evolution we have agreed with Kant that truth is basically unknowable. The result of such a doctrine is the ultimate abolition of truth, for which a general, noncommital approach is substituted.

At the end of the century a definite step towards political unity in Europe is to be brought about by the monetary union (EU). The European Union, as a supra-national organization with its gigantic bureaucracy, is a classical example of the double-entity state. Government policy and economic power are disastrously welded together.

The EU, through its marketing organization, which is a means of controlling agricultural production through money, has got nearly the whole of European agriculture under its control. By means of financial supremacy everyone and everything is dependent on it to the detriment of nature and mankind. As a small example of barely conceivable absurdities, we would mention that there is now a course of studies in the agricultural field that is devoted to a special training for the effective exploitation of EU subsidies! Government subsidies as management of agricultural production. In this connection it sounds like a prophetic warning when Solovyev in his story *The Antichrist* portrays the president of the United States of Europe as this Antichrist. It is really necessary to look at Europeans and their community life from a different angle than that of the EU, which does not overcome the principle of the centralized state but intensifies it.

## *The tragedy of the Threefold Social Order as the form appropriate to Christ*

As mentioned earlier, the importance of the spiritual life for the threefold social organism will here be explained more fully; for in looking back over the past century, the extensive tragedy of its rejection is made clear. To begin with, Rudolf Steiner saw the 'true form of the social question' primarily in the ideological character assumed by spiritual life — especially that of the proletariat of his day.

> People's thoughts in this respect will undergo a complete change, when once they come really to feel the full weight of this fact: that, in a human community where spiritual life plays a merely ideological role, common social life lacks one of the forces that can make and keep it a living organism. What ails the body social today is impotence of spiritual life. And the disease is aggravated by the reluctance to acknowledge its existence. Once the fact is acknowledged there will then be a basis on which to develop the kind of thinking needed for the social movement.[78]

At the end of the century one would have to comment sarcastically: 'We have come to the conclusion that the illness does not exist, it was an illusion; basically everything is in the best of health.'

The way in which the ideological character of spiritual life can be overcome is expressed by Rudolf Steiner in relation to the 'proletarian'—today it would be generally applicable—as follows.

'He sees nothing of the workings of an actual reality behind these branches of the spiritual life [science, religion, morality, rights], which finds its way into his own human ideology.'[79]

In another place it is made even clearer:

'If we discover anywhere a life of the soul arising out of the forces of the present age, rooted in spiritual reality and able to sustain humanity—then such a soul life as this could radiate the power needed to lead the social movement in the right direction.'[80]

From a spiritual life deserving of the name a power must go forth which can 'sustain man's soul and give him a consciousness of his human worth'.[81]

The spiritual life that Rudolf Steiner characterized was for him the living source for the whole of the social organism. This source flows out of the reality of the spiritual world, which is freely available from spiritually productive people. So the social question is primarily one of spiritual reality, without which the problems cannot be solved.

Later expositions by Rudolf Steiner draw a direct connection between the tasks of spiritual life and the Christ-impulse.

> A social community in the name of Christ will however be possible, providing we do not insist on a political state, but rather establish an independent life of the spirit. This can be Christian through and through. And this independent life of the spirit will be able to illumine the sphere of life

where we have government and states, a sphere that simply cannot be Christian. The result will be that an economic life based on associations can develop, though this, too, cannot be Christian in itself. The people who are involved in it will be Christian, however. They will be filled with the Christ-impulse. What we must do is to let people enter into an independent life of the spirit. Then it will be possible to make the whole of social life Christian.[82]

From the quotation which follows it can be seen in what a wide perspective Rudolf Steiner foresaw the Threefold Commonwealth, also in connection with the Christ Event of the twentieth century:

The abstract ideal of brotherhood or companionship must become something real. How can companionship become real? By associating, by truly uniting with the other person, by no longer fighting people with different interests but instead combining those different interests. Associations are the living embodiment of companionship. The life-spirit must be alive in the sphere of rights, and with the Christ Spirit brought into economic life, spirit-man will come to life in its first beginnings through associations. The earth, however, yields none of this. Human beings will only come to this if they let the Christ, who is now approaching the ether, enter their hearts and minds and souls.[83]

Through the 'spiritual renewal of the Mystery of Golgotha' man will find the strength to bear within himself 'the potential to develop spirit-self, life-spirit and spirit-man' so that these start to become a reality in the spirit life, the life of rights and the economic life. The emerging future trinity of man needs the Threefold Social Order as its social structure. 'The true life of the spirit exists only where it is strong enough to overcome material life — and not leave it to one side as something that enslaves and compels us.'[84]

A further requirement for the Threefold Social Order is presented by the threshold experience of humanity. The passing of the Threshold requires the separation of thinking, feeling and willing within the soul. That is heralded in the individual by an often observed instability of the soul and in 'split-personality' traits. The social organism must correspond to humanity by being divided into three in order to absorb the forces that result from the transit into the spiritual world. Just as the individual 'I' needs to be strengthened by the power of the Christ for the crossing of the Threshold, so does the social organism need the form through which the Christ Event of the century can work.

Just as man, the knower, must realize that his thinking, feeling and willing separate in a certain sense, and that he must hold them together at a higher level, so it must be made intelligible to modern humanity that the spiritual life, the life of rights and the economic life must separate from each other and a higher form of union than the present state be created. No programmes, ideas or ideologies of any kind can make individuals recognize the necessity of a threefold social organism. Thorough knowledge of the progressive evolution of mankind alone reveals to us that this evolution has reached a Threshold where a stern Guardian stands. This Guardian demands of an individual who is advancing to higher knowledge: Submit to the separation between thinking, feeling and willing! And of humanity as a whole he demands: Separate what has hitherto been interwoven in chaotic unity in the idolized, centralized state; separate this into a spiritual life, an equity sphere, an economic sphere. Otherwise no progress is possible for humanity, and the old chaos will burst asunder, will go to pieces. But if that happens it will not take the form that is necessary for the good of humanity; it will have an ahrimanic or luciferic form. The knowledge acquired from spiritual science of the crossing of the Threshold in our present time, can alone give the form that is truly Christlike.[85]

At the end of the century this solemn demand by the Guardian of the Threshold can confront the soul, laying the 'form appropriate to Christ' of the social organism upon its heart. This 'form appropriate to Christ' bears hidden within itself healing, restorative, consecrating forces for the future that come from the spiritual world, for in this figure akin to Christ lies the force of attraction for the good spirits of mankind, for that which we can rightly call blessing. Over against that the centralized state, in all its forms in the twentieth century, shows a greater or lesser affinity to the various evil spirits.

In respect of the present century the 'form appropriate to Christ' of the social organism can only be preserved in the consciousness, the heart and the will of those people who recognize its real significance for the social life of mankind.

Tragedy confronts the spiritual gaze. It could not have been otherwise. And yet, a genuine spiritual chance has been thrown away—a contradiction, a paradox. Has something like a further Crucifixion of Christ taken place in our century because this Christ-appropriate form could not be accepted?

## *Mammon and Halley's Comet (1910/1986)*

An event that plays a significant role in relation to the end of the century—as to the whole of the Michael Age and the distant future—is connected by Rudolf Steiner with the start of the 'radiant dominion of Michael'. 'Today already, at the same time as Michael, a dark god has begun his regency: the god Mammon. In the sense of occultism Mammon is not only the god of money.'[86]

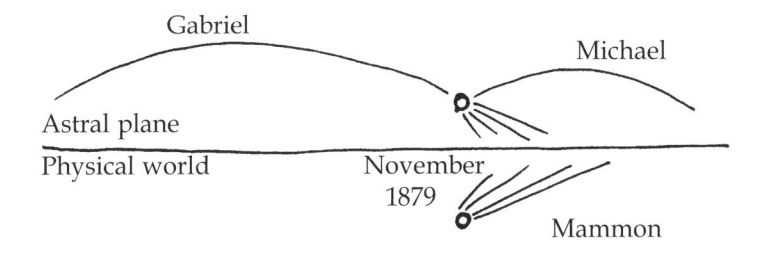

## SORATH RAISES HIS HEAD AT THE END OF THE CENTURY 69

```
                 Gabriel
         _____                    Michael
                              ○_____
Astral plane                   ⦀⦀⦀
_____
Physical world            November ⦀⦀
                            1879   ⦀⦀
                                 ○
                                    Mammon
```

The point of view which holds that 'Mammon is the god of money' must be brought to our consciousness, although in view of the situation of our time, we do not need to comment on the strength of Mammon. But it is important to remember that the rule of Michael is, so to say, accompanied by the terrestrial and sub-earthly forces of Mammon. Mammon's resistance, which is necessary for the development of consciousness, has to be taken into account by those who wish to connect themselves with the Michael impulses. It is of course clear that the impulses of the dark god Mammon lie in the direction of Ahriman and Sorath. He appears as the servant of both.

It cannot of course be a question here of the commonplace everyday wisdom that gold rules the world. In a certain sense it has always done that. The betrayal by Judas was paid for with 30 pieces of silver, which demonstrates Mammon's involvement in it.

Here we are only concerned with the methods employed by Mammon since 1879. What particular role does Mammon play in the twentieth century? Which one at the present day? It has already been pointed out that the 'unrestrained incurring of debt' by the state was regarded by the German resistance fighters as the work of Hitler from 1933 onwards.[87]

The incurring of debts has since become a universally accepted government policy, which is not seriously questioned even though the consequences are catastrophic. The power of money has risen enormously through the trick by which all states are fairly unrestrained in getting into further and further debt, because they have got themselves hopelessly entangled in capitalism. Investors do not need to fear bankruptcy and the consequent loss of their money because, in spite of actual bankruptcy, to which politics has actually led, bankruptcy of the state is inconceivable. The existence of the centralized state, which is never called into question, supports and perpetuates, so to speak, the power of money; and the power of money, for its part, supports the state.

If the statesmen had been unable to incur fresh debts again and again under all kinds of pretexts, they would all long ago have been at their wits' end. That is not recognized by the general public, which is both the beneficiary and the paymaster. An immense, unnoticed exploitation is taking place to the advantage of the capitalist. It is no comfort for the public to participate in it through the capital they possess, for the strangulating effect of the process is not thereby alleviated, as the rising—sometimes sinking—revenue has to be used in paying interest.

Since the eighties, i.e. a hundred years after the beginning of Mammon's rulership, this process has steadily increased. To it belongs the shameless triumph of capitalism since 1989, through which a high—but hopefully in the end not too high—price was paid for the freeing of East Germany. The future appears to belong to money. It has become the regulator of all social processes—something which runs of its own accord. Total commercialization is the order of the day for the god Mammon, money being the absolute ruler; everything is purchasable, even esotericism. Schiller's frivolous remark (from *Fiesco*) appears to be turning into reality: 'Ignominy diminishes as sin increases.' Commerce drives to excesses. It has become well known in the meantime that humanity has been given the so-called mad-cow disease (BSE) as a result of commercial considerations, from wrongly feeding a meat diet to cattle. Less well known is the fact that just such a commercial reason led to 125,000 bee colonies being destroyed in Mecklenburg. Examples are endless.

The new quality—if one can so term it—in the management of money appears in processes that would have been considered impossible a short while ago. Money can be earned more quickly and in greater amounts through investing it than by entrepreneurial activity. People are made redundant even in spite of increasing profits in some cases. The capping of workforce wages is demanded in spite of the fact that the managers' income and profits are rising. The profit achieved by this means can then be immediately reinvested.

The god Mammon produces immense illusions. In the reality of a healthy social organism, money is only a symbol representing the value of goods and services carried out. To that extent money is of no value in itself. It is maya, even though Mammon continually repeats his great lie, 'money works'; for this sort of 'work' lends money a certain reality. Only man can carry out work; Mammon's lie puts money above humankind, which is a characteristic of present-day society. But also through the fact that ownership of land and the right to ownership of the means of production is valued in terms of cash, money gains a power to which it is not entitled by right of its function.

The idea of interest, which springs from the inner being of Mammon (not altogether wrong by reason of that), has the tendency to enhance the position of money enormously and lend it the nonsensical appearance of power that it has today.[88]

On the whole one can clearly perceive the intention of Mammon—as in Ahriman and Sorath—to give a (false) reality to what is merely thought out.

This comes to expression through the fact that the anonymity of capital suppresses the individuality ever more and more. Decision and responsibility are delegated to Mammon in growing measure.[89] Through Mammon man has devised a money system which excludes himself.

The question arises as to how far the acceleration of Mammon's development is connected with the second appearance of Halley's Comet in the present century (1985/86).[90] At any rate, however, Halley's Comet is a cosmic phenomenon which is connected to the reappearance of Christ. Rudolf Steiner first spoke about Halley's Comet in 1910 in connection with the greatest event of the twentieth century.[91] The influence of this comet affects the 'I' so that it becomes more closely attached to the physical body, especially the brain. That fulfils a necessary, beneficial task in the history of mankind, ensuring that the 'I' is connected more firmly with the earth. However it acquires a dangerous materialistic character when this process of evolution comes to an end, as it did with the appearance of the comet in 1835. For the twentieth century, therefore, the effects become the reverse of what they had been before.

In the present year 1910 we are experiencing a new appearance of the ancient comet, and that signifies a year of crisis in respect to the view just discussed. All the forces are at work there to give birth to a still shallower and worse sense in the human soul, to create a materialistic 'bog'. Man is placed before a mighty test, a trial to determine whether, alongside the threat of deepest descent, the impulse to ascend can prevail. For otherwise it would not be possible for man to overcome the resistance which the materialistic view puts in his way. If man were not exposed to materialism, he would not be able to overcome it out of his own forces. And now the opportunity is offered him to choose between the spiritual and the materialistic path. The terms for this year of crisis are sent us from the cosmos.[92]

The 'impulse for ascent' as opposed to the 'threatened deepest descent' was given by Rudolf Steiner in the year of the comet 1910 when he spoke in various towns on his way from Stockholm to Rome about the etheric reappearance of Christ, without doubt so that the strongest forces of opposition could be awakened in man in our century. The strongest force of opposition is decidedly necessary, for Rudolf Steiner on another occasion draws attention to the fact that the next trial of mankind by this comet—the one in 1985/1986—will present us with greater demands, because for 76 years the opportunity will have been there for spiritual activity to prepare for it. How seriously this second trial was regarded by Rudolf Steiner is made clear by his remark that by failing the test mankind could sink lower than the level it occupied during Kali Yuga.[93] Already the formulation 'the materialistic bog' chosen by him to describe 1910 speaks for itself. At any rate it is clear that in the many-layered and varied processes around the end of the century, a role is also played by the passing or failing of the test provided by Halley's Comet.

It must be left to each individual to observe the symptoms of our time and decide what kind of reality we have actually come to inhabit.

## *Ahriman's forthcoming incarnation*

The awaited incarnation of Ahriman in the West is rightly seen as being connected with the end of the century, or better said the end of the millennium. In order to prevail in the present test, it is essential to distinguish between Ahriman and Sorath. Sorath does not himself incarnate but he helps in every way he can to promote the incarnation of Ahriman. Solovyev, in his story of the Antichrist, has portrayed the relationship of these two in a graphic manner. The Superman, the prospective Antichrist, is so full of self-love that he is unable and unwilling to acknowledge the divinity and the Resurrection of Christ. So his whole being is filled with a 'burning envy and fury which seizes and contracts all his being and fills his soul with hate'.[94] He feels Christ's pity for him and flings himself into the abyss, because he cannot bear it. But he is preserved from this end and sees 'a figure, bright with phosphorescent misty radiance' before him.

> He saw its two piercing eyes and heard, proceeding neither from within nor from without, a strange voice, dull, as if smothered, and at the same time precise and entirely soulless, as if it came from a gramophone. The voice said to him: 'My well-beloved son, all my affection is in thee. Why hast thou not sought me? Why honour that other, the wicked One and His Father. I am God and thy father! The other—a beggar and crucified One—is a stranger to me and to thee. I have no other son but thee. Thou my only, only begotten, equal to me, I love thee and ask nothing of thee. For thou art so beautiful, great and powerful. Act in thine own name, not in mine. I do not envy thee; I love thee. I am in need of nothing from thee. He whom thou didst deem a god, demanded of His Son obedience and boundless subservience, and He was unable to help Him on the Cross. I require nothing of thee, and I shall help thee.[95]

Difference and unity are here portrayed in masterly fashion. The self-love of the now incarnated Antichrist is increased immeasurably through renunciation of obedience. The Antichrist in this case is Ahriman, not Sorath, who as it were remains hidden and says: 'Receive my Spirit!' The impulse of the Antichrist unites the two beings here represented.

Man's powers of recognition are challenged by Ahriman to the utmost, both prior to and also during his incarnation. Man has to recognize Ahriman for what he is and then decide what to accept from him and what to learn. This knowledge-process develops man's powers of judgement to overcome many mistakes. If he cannot recognize Ahriman, he succumbs to him, even when he thinks he has to reject him lock, stock and barrel. Man only fulfils his task with regard to Ahriman when he recognizes him. Even though Ahriman advances his own anonymity in all possible ways, he still suffers some loss when he is not recognized. In a distant future Christ will be able to redeem Ahriman.

It is different in the case of Sorath, whose impulse must also be recognized by man who, however, cannot learn or accept anything from him. We are, instead, much more called to a decision of will, to one between the black and the white path of initiation. That has an essentially different quality than the one we can attain to by recognizing and transforming ahrimanic forces. As a result of the special constellation connected with the activity of Sorath at the end of the century, the impulses of the latter merge with those preparing Ahriman's incarnation. The fact that these preparations are in full swing and yet are hardly recognized is a direct result of the explanation given above.

With that, however, nothing has been said about the timing of the incarnation. This question has been dealt with recently by Hans Peter van Manen in an article in *Das Goetheanum* entitled 'The incarnation of the adversarial powers as Rudolf Steiner saw it—the time of Ahriman's incarnation'.[96] Through a thorough and balanced review of all relevant statements by Rudolf Steiner on this question, Hans Peter van Manen arrives at the conclusion that this incarnation of Ahriman will take place 'either at the beginning of the third millennium—that could mean right at the beginning of the twenty-first century—or still earlier! The latter would mean that the incarnation-process would already start earlier, that is, during the last years of the twentieth century, in order to reach its culmination and end in the first years of the twenty-first century.'[97] Hans Peter van Manen arrives at this statement through a subtle assessment of Rudolf Steiner's statement: 'Just as there was an incarnation of Lucifer in the flesh and an incarnation of Christ in the flesh, so, before only a part of the third millennium of the post-Christian era has elapsed, there will be, in the West, an actual incarnation of Ahriman: Ahriman in the flesh.'[98]

Hans Peter van Manen convincingly emphasizes his view by pointing to the fact that Lucifer developed his activity in the third millennium BC and that Ahriman will develop his in the third millennium AD. That signifies, however, that if a balance is to be achieved around the central event, 3000–2000 BC must correspond to AD 2000–3000. This point of view also connects the incarnation of Ahriman with the end of the millennium.

Just as important, however, are the symptoms that are recognizable in the continuing and intensifying preparations that Ahriman is making for his incarnation. Hans Peter van Manen summarizes these characteristics under eight headings (e.g. the increase of nationalism, the splitting into parties, Jesus being regarded as only human, belief in numbers and statistics, study methods used in universities), which more or less correspond to the above-mentioned characteristics of Sorath's method of working. But, common to both of them, is that these in general are all largely acknowledged or accepted, and that questions about them have ceased to be asked. From that we can draw conclusions about the intensity of the preparations, and recognize that at the best only a small circle of people is adequately prepared for Ahriman's incarnation.

Let me just mention that what carries most weight in this context is the fact that 'if the old centralized state as such — whether a democracy, a republic, a monarchy, or whatever — does not become *threefold*, this promotes Ahriman's incarnation.'[99]

In the social sphere the centralized state corresponds to the Old Adam within man, which serves as a vessel for

Sorath. This centralized state prepares the way for Ahriman's incarnation because it cannot be recognized as a danger and therefore cannot be overcome. Sorath and Ahriman behave towards one another in this connection as Solovyev describes it.

Rudolf Steiner has indicated that he had to refrain from referring directly to the beings and interconnections underlying the threefold social state.

> Today people cannot hear the plain unadorned truth, which they would deride, make fun of and scorn. However, if one gives it them, as was attempted through the Threefold Commonwealth, then they still do not want it, at least not the majority. But the fact that people do not want such things is just one of the facts which serve the ahrimanic powers, so that when Ahriman incarnates in human form he will have the greatest number of supporters on the earth. Just this rejection of the most important truths will provide Ahriman with the best bridge for the success of his incarnation.[100]

The attainment of the goal of the earth depends upon the greatest possible number of people passing the test set by the incarnation of Ahriman. In so far as Sorath raises his head at the end of the century and paves the way for Ahriman, the human and earthly future actually depends on how strongly mankind can brace itself, by conscious recognition, to voluntary opposition. The following words of Rudolf Steiner about Ahriman's incarnation can give us a strong motivation:

> From the spiritual world this ahrimanic power is preparing for its incarnation on the earth, is endeavouring in every conceivable way to make such preparation that the incarnation of its human form may be able to mislead and corrupt mankind on earth to the uttermost. A task of mankind during the next phase of civilization will be to

live towards the incarnation of Ahriman with such alert consciousness that this incarnation can actually serve to promote a higher, spiritual development, inasmuch as through Ahriman himself man will become aware of what can, or shall we say, can *not* be achieved by physical life alone. But people must go forward with full consciousness towards this incarnation of Ahriman and become more and more alert in every domain, in order to recognize with greater and greater clarity those trends in life which are leading towards this ahrimanic incarnation. Human beings must learn from spiritual science to find the key to life and so be able to recognize and learn to control the currents leading towards the incarnation of Ahriman. It must be realized that Ahriman will live among people on the earth, but that in confronting him people will themselves determine what they may learn from him, what they may receive from him. This, however, they will not be able to do unless, from now onwards, they take control of certain spiritual and also unspiritual currents which otherwise are used by Ahriman for the purpose of leaving mankind as deeply unconscious as possible of his coming. Then, one day, he will be able to appear on earth and overwhelm human beings, tempting and luring them to repudiate Earth evolution, thus preventing it from reaching its goal.[101]

The importance of the end of the century cannot be stated too emphatically. In order for Sorath, the Sun Demon and Antichrist, to be able to drive souls *en masse* into the arms of Lucifer and Ahriman, the dark spirits of Ahriman and Mammon congregate around him, serving him and at the same time receiving spiritual strength from him. Each, individually and collectively, wishes to cover up the spiritual aspect of Christ who approaches mankind by coming to the very threshold of the spiritual world.

# 6
# Coming to Terms with the Apocalyptic Beast

*'Watch and pray!'*

The following statement by Rudolf Steiner can contribute a great deal towards understanding the present century and also gaining the right attitude in the manifold situations which we encounter: 'Our age is in many respects a renewal of those times which came about partly as a result of the Mystery of Golgotha, partly because of what happened in AD 333 and partly through the events of 666.'[102]

Therewith is indicated that the new Christ Event of the twentieth century is placed into the world in a similar way to the Christ Event at the turn of the era. For a start mankind refuses to accept the Christ Event. That is exemplified in the crassest fashion by the rejection of the Threefold Social Order; then it is further demonstrated by the opposition this Christ Event receives from recalcitrant spiritual beings and their human servants. The small and great Caesars are present and so is the madness of the Caesars, through which man poses as God, or by which he is tempted to gain power over other people. Those who were physically present when Christ walked the earth and were His disciples, as also those who lived at the time of early Christianity, wondered how they should respond towards the events which took place in the Roman Empire. 'Render unto Caesar the things that are Caesar's,' Christ said to them. That could have been understood then as it still can be today to mean that Christians should neither flee nor fall prey. As contemporaries we should not run away from nor be afraid of what comes to us unavoidably at the present time, but we should also not participate in everything we encounter. It is easy for us to be led by our fellow human beings to become the children of our age by yielding to the powers of decadence. Innumerable individual situations necessitate that we should make decisions that call on our discrimination. The call which resounded in the decadent Roman Empire, *panem et circenses* (bread and games), can be detected today in a modern form in the consumer society which takes possession of the will, and the media which occupy the mind in a more or less sensational way as an onlooker.

There was a clear boundary for the early Christians. If they had to acknowledge Caesar as a God, they would rather face death by letting themselves be eaten by the lions in the circus or by standing as living torches in Nero's garden. Those who testified to the living Christ-experience suffered martyrdom. In the twentieth century everyone must decide where his own boundary lies, which can only be determined through each person's individual experience of Christ. Where there is no boundary, the Christ experience has not become fully conscious by imbuing the whole human being. The beginnings of spiritual consciousness direct man along the road towards the Spirit of the Age, to Michael, through whom perception and thinking is united with the willing of the Christ-impulse.

A full hundred years ago Friedrich Nietzsche was what Rudolf Steiner, in his book about him, calls 'a fighter for freedom', or a fighter against the time in which he lived. That is an ideal, and through the Nietzsche destiny we are warned of the threatened dangers that lurk wherever the consciousness becomes dulled. A 'fighter against the time in which he lived' does not mean that he fights against the people of his time. Through the Christ-impulse we stand in connection with everything human; nothing is alien, nothing is excluded. But one must try to become conscious of what is active in man, both of evil and of good.

When Christ appeared as Man at the turn of the era in Roman occupied Palestine, this event was in the truest sense only of marginal significance to the Roman Empire, although the future depended on it. It remained unnoticed, disregarded, and played no part in the public consciousness to such an extent that—happily—it was not historically recorded. Only a handful of people could grasp what proceeded from Christ and were able to tend it, because their souls were touched and their hearts were warmed. In this respect, too, the early Christian era is similar to our own, for when—especially in the case of the Threefold Social Movement—the spiritual possibility was present for a larger community of people to be drawn towards anthroposophy, the fact remains that by the end of the century only a tiny section of humanity (in comparison with the number of living people) seriously devote themselves to anthroposophy. This does not in any way affect the correct assertion that, in contrast to the time of Christ, a very much greater number of people have the impulse for anthroposophy slumbering within them. Whatever may have been the cause for this impulse not to have been awakened, this small group of people can only increase in numbers as a result of such awakening. So the call goes out today, 'Unite with the smallest party' (from Goethe's poem *Vermächtnis* [Testament]). To this handful of upright folk only those belong who consciously and actively determine to take issue against the multifarious evil forces with the help of spiritual science. And any kind of false arrogance which might result will only arise in someone who does not feel the tremendous sense of responsibility involved in being the lynchpin for the whole of humanity. This maintaining of equilibrium need not be on a vast scale; and though one may feel overtaxed and overwhelmed by the responsibility, the important thing nevertheless is to remain steadfast.

Whoever feels akin to this handful of steadfast ones will experience the reality of this union by the fact that he is thrown back upon his own ego. Only then has the sphere been attained in which one can come to grips with the apocalyptic Beast. A whole series of events then takes place, of which only two can be mentioned here. The one experience is loneliness, isolation, desertion, of which Morgenstern makes mention when he says: 'Those who set out towards truth, do so alone!' And Mephisto asks Faust who set out towards the Mothers: 'Hast thou a notion of solitude and deserts?' (Goethe: *Faust*, Part II, Act I, 'A Gloomy Gallery'). For the ego is thrown back completely on itself in this sphere.

The other experience is arrived at through the strict resoluteness which the 'I' imposes on itself and through which, as a last resort, it is enabled to sacrifice itself. Examples of what is meant here can be found in individual destinies such as those of Count Helmuth James von Moltke (executed 1945), Albrecht Haushofer (shot 1945) and Ken Saro-Wiwa, who was put to death on 10 November 1995 in Nigeria with his eight companions.[103]

In the sphere of the 'I' the question can now be asked: 'How do I find the Christ?' The answer to this question contains at the same time a confrontation with Sorath. The way to Christ which can be traversed by the ego is conditioned by something that belongs to a time before birth. It is described by Rudolf Steiner as follows:

> Just as those who were contemporaries of the Mystery of Golgotha only reached full understanding of it centuries later, so we ourselves experience a kind of reflected picture of an experience we had long before—hundreds of years before we were born. This applies to people of the present time only. All of them, when they are born into the physical world, bring with them something that is like a reflected picture of the Mystery of Golgotha, a mirror-image of what they experienced in the spiritual world in the centuries after the Mystery of Golgotha.
>
> Naturally, this impulse cannot be directly perceived by one who has not supersensible vision; but all human beings can experience its effect within themselves.[104]

In order to have this experience the following is necessary:

We find the Christ only when we have the following experiences. Firstly, we must say to ourselves: 'I will strive for *self-knowledge* as far as in me lies, as far as my whole human personality makes this possible.' Now nobody who strives honestly for self-knowledge today can fail to come to the conclusion that he is incapable of laying hold of that for which he is striving, that his power of comprehension lags behind his striving. He feels the ineffectiveness of his efforts. This is a very real experience. A certain feeling of ineffectiveness is experienced by everyone who in the quest for self-knowledge takes honest counsel with himself. It is a wholesome feeling, for it is nothing else than awareness of the sickness in us; and when we have an illness without being aware of it, then we are all the more ill. In feeling at some point in our life the powerlessness to lift ourselves to the Divine, we become aware of that sickness of which I have spoken, the sickness that has been implanted into us. And in becoming aware of this sickness, we feel that, as the body is today, our soul would be condemned to die with it.

When this powerlessness is experienced with sufficient intensity, there comes the sudden reversal—the other experience which tells us that if we do not depend only upon what our bodily forces by themselves enable us to achieve, but devote ourselves to what the spirit gives, we can overcome this inner death of the soul. We find our soul again and unite ourselves with the spirit. We can experience the futility of existence on the one side and, on the other, the triumph of it within ourselves, when we have overcome the feeling of helplessness. We can be aware of the sickness, the powerlessness that has become allied with death in our soul, and then of the redemptive, healing force. And then we feel that we bear in our soul something that can at all times rise above death. It is in seeking for these two experiences that we find the Christ in our own soul.

Humanity is approaching this experience. Angelus Silesius spoke of it in the significant words:

> In vain the Cross on Golgotha
> Was raised—thou hast not any part
> In its deliverance unless
> It be raised up within thy heart.

It is raised up in man when he is conscious of the two poles: powerlessness through the body, resurrection through the spirit.[105]

In experiencing this powerlessness two things are essential. On the one hand it becomes clear to the one who is undergoing the experience that it is only through this feeling of powerlessness that one can be led to Christ, in other words, that Christ is only to be found in a realm beyond power, a realm in which every claim to power must have been renounced before one can enter the sphere of freedom that lives in Christ. Therewith it also becomes clear that the power which manifests today at every level of life is centred in Sorath. On the other hand it is also evident that this powerlessness is the result of the illness, the 'kink', the 'thorn in the flesh', which has remained behind from the activity of Sorath in the physical body. Sorath himself is experienced by man through his (Sorath's) representatives. It is in the sense of the paradox mentioned in Chapter 1 that the 'reversal' comes about. That is the decisive point in the overcoming of Sorath. There is a strong force in man which wants to avoid this experience because it resembles a kind of inner burning process, which is not easily recognized as a purgation. But Sorath is helped if we do not subject ourselves to it. The soul becomes inventive in finding all possible and impossible pretexts to recoil from it. Rudolf Steiner draws attention to its main cause:

> It is a happening in regard to which the excuse of lacking faculties of supersensible perception is not valid. Such faculties are not essential. All that is essential is to be resolute in the practice of self-examination and to have the will to overcome the attitude of self-sufficiency which is so prevalent today, and which prevents man from realizing that insistence upon placing reliance solely in his own faculties is a result of pride.[106]

This temptation is the greater because cowardice and indolence are hidden under a cloak of modesty.

The process of change, however, is only possible as a result of supersensible preparation.

> For this experience is the recovery of what we experienced in the spiritual world hundreds of years before our birth. We must seek here, on the physical plane, for its mirror-image in the soul. Seek within yourselves and you will discover the powerlessness! Seek, and you will find, after the experience of powerlessness, the redemption from it, the resurrection of the soul to the spirit.[107]

This 'resurrection of the soul to the spirit' is the true refutation of the abolition of the spirit decreed by the Council of 869, which came about through Sorath. Christ Himself must contradict the doctrine of His Church. At the same time the way is shown along which healing can truly be sought for the manifold sickness of the soul.

The 'resurrection of the soul to the spirit' has its consequences. What appears to be the result, but also aids, supports and helps the process, circulates in a living flow. Those are activities of the 'I' which oppose the work of Sorath and Ahriman.

A real interest in the present age and in one's fellow human beings combats the soul-sleep which has overcome humanity. Whoever consciously experiences the stupefying effect of the present time is enabled to change it into an active acceptance of events. For that it is necessary to maintain a connection to people with whom one is karmically bound, and just as freely to engage in new connections. The forming of relationships, however inconspicuous, leads on into the future.

The 'I' is closely bound up with conscience, whose voice becomes deeper, but whose impulses are not easily made conscious enough. Nevertheless conscience, which a person must obey irrespective of outside judgement, is an ultimate expression of the ego. The greatest achievements of the present century are due to the conscious decisions made by ego-imbued personalities. In close connection with that is the resistance which has to be exerted in the sense of the battle against the present age, against trends and majorities and lies. Boundaries must be drawn, so that we are not swayed by falsehood. By saying 'no' we can be protected from being drawn into unlimited and senseless conflict. The constant trial of the ego consists in the first place of not deluding ourselves, but of squarely facing the truths that arise out of the study of spiritual science. The consciousness for truth can only be nurtured by an ever-renewed, consciously developed seriousness.

Whatever one does, or omits to do, one will have to admit that one's doings or omissions are not without mistakes. These may be caused by a wrong assessment or by the necessity of a hasty decision, or perhaps by both of these together. A person who is imbued with the truth of future lives on earth will be able to say to himself that he has the gallant intention to accept responsibility for his deeds or omissions throughout his future life and destiny. Through that he takes on himself a great responsibility which, if properly understood, gives him the motivation for his actions. Along such soul-paths as this, a person takes issue, in many ways and on various levels, against the evil beings who continually wish to divert him from his goal.

In order to survive the encounter with the Beast it is also necessary to undertake a conscious training of thinking, feeling and willing. To tread this path in earnestness and with perseverance and patience demands a high degree of consciousness and strength of will, because the will of Sorath is opposed to it.

In spite of wakeful consciousness the soul slumbers in thinking, because the access to reality of its processes is blocked by the mirroring character of the concepts. That is the true basis of the 'epidemic loss of reality' (Golo Mann) of the present day. The soul-sleep can only be overcome by the study of spiritual science.

> One is able to study spiritual science today, it exists, one really has no need to do anything but study spiritual science. If, in addition, one were to carry out all sorts of meditations, if one were to take into consideration such practical suggestions as are given in *Knowledge of the Higher Worlds: How is it Achieved?*, one would support the matter still further. But the essentials are met when one just studies spiritual science and understands it really consciously. One can study spiritual science today without acquiring clairvoyant faculties; everyone can do so if he does not himself put prejudices in the way. And if people were to study spiritual science more and more, if they were to acquire concepts and ideas given by spiritual science, their consciousness would awaken to such an extent that certain events would not go unnoticed, but be consciously perceived.[108]

One has to take into account that the study of spiritual science represents the first step towards higher knowledge, towards initiation, and that this study consists of reading books and lectures only as the first stage.[109] The study of spiritual science entails continued pondering on spiritual ideas, having the courage to face one's own doubts and antagonisms, conscious contemplation of reasons and counter-reasons, the testing of statements and results by their fruitfulness for life, and an implacable research for truth. One arrives at a gradual understanding if one is prepared to radically acknowledge one's lack of understanding and thereby become conscious of it. Study is connected with biographical development, because it concerns the whole human being and one is reassured by the fact that what has been achieved consciously is continually forgotten and passes into the state of sleep in which one is every night immersed in the depths of world reality. On the basis of the study of spiritual science, that which one's ego has consciously striven for rises up, so to speak, out of the depths of the unconscious during the course of one's life, but now in a form that gives assurance to the 'I' through this authentication process of the truth. The 'I' knows then that it is on the right path; the first step of the awakening has taken place.

It is of the greatest significance for this development of the 'I' to take up the various aspects of spiritual science and to come to terms with the apparent discrepancies. There is nothing which activates the 'I' more than a conscious involvement in the most varied points of view, each of which is a different cosmic aspect. The study of spiritual science leads to a well-founded trust in the unfolding of thought, and allows a person access to the spiritual world without him having to first develop clairvoyance.

The study of spiritual science is naturally not just a development of the thinking but, above all, an unfolding and cultivation of feeling and willing. Along the pathways of feeling the way leads to the experience of the processes and beings of the world, to an awareness of what weaves between things. Indolence of heart can only be overcome by the enkindling of sympathy.

On the path of knowledge the most intensive struggle

takes place in the will. It has been described how Sorath wants to tear the individual ego, the bearer of karma, out of the will, because in the will resides the actual ego itself, not merely its concept as in ordinary thinking. The sorathic powers work upon the will in such a way that paralysis, resignation, lack of commitment and *laissez-faire* are produced as preliminary stages of a direct attack upon the 'I'. The person who is paralysed in the will is an observer of the world, who allows its pictures to pass before his gaze in a playful and frivolous manner without participation on his part. He has lost the motive which drives him on to action. Deeds without motive, that is to say, deeds which show no direct and concrete link between perpetrator and victim (e.g. bombing raids) therefore are characteristic of Sorath's way of working, for the ego lives in the motive. Therefore Sorath works against motives which are taken up by the will to bring about actions. The simplest, and here most significant, example of this is that of embarking on the path of exercises. If this path should lead to serious and lasting work, then the appeal to the ego in the will produces a tendency for it to ascend into consciousness. The patient practising of exercises brings about a strengthening and consolidation of the will and makes it capable of withstanding the dangers with which Sorath threatens it.

The exercises that are given in the Foundation Stone of the Anthroposophical Society to lead to a proper thinking, feeling and willing summarize what will make a person so strong that he is able to cope with the encounter with the apocalyptic Beast. For of the thinking that takes hold of the 'spirit's universal thoughts' it is said, '*In the spirit's universal thoughts the soul awakens.*' The feeling finds the '*Christ Will in the encircling rounds in the rhythms of the worlds, blessing the soul*' and comes to the experience which is expressed in the words: '*In Christ death becomes Life*'. The will consorts with the '*Father Spirit of the Heights*', who holds sway in the '*Depths of worlds begetting Life*' in the correct relationship. He remains bound fast to the original being of mankind which lives in the words: *'From God mankind has Being'*.[110] If the spirituality of this trinity lives in man, Sorath will have no hold over him.

All kinds of outward show at the end of the century must not mislead one into overlooking the fact that the combined forces of wicked beings are driving mankind towards the abyss, towards non-existence.[111] What is old in the world is destined for destruction, so that, by experiencing the destruction, strength is engendered to grasp what is new with courage. Thus mankind encounters the void into which the evil beings would plunge it. But if the ego can withstand this encounter, the sight of the void is changed into the Threshold of the spiritual world, before which the Guardian is standing. He who learns this truth can oppose Sorath—as Faust does Mephisto before his visit to the Mothers—with the words, 'In this thy Nothing, may I find my All!' (Goethe: *Faust*, Part II, Act I, 'A Gloomy Gallery'), because he is imbued with the certainty that beyond the threshold lies the spiritual world.

The indispensable recognition and true naming of the apocalyptic Beast and the experiencing of the unfathomable depths of evil which would destroy man's ego develop a capacity in us to prevail in the encounter with the Beast. By holding out against the sight of evil when encountered face to face, strength is gained to overcome Sorath. The victory over evil leads to the conscious choice of the ego for Christ. Through that the Christ Event of the twentieth century can be apprehended by the 'I'.

# 7
# *The Christ Event of the Twentieth Century*

This time of consciousness-soul development and the Age of Michael is a time of awakening to the spirit of man's ego. So from the start, the Christ Event is an individual, intimate and stirring event for every person who experiences it. In addition this experience is one of freedom on both sides. The conscious choice of the ego for Christ, indicated above, is only conceivable as an act of free will. The Christ experience always bears the character of intuition, of grace; it does not allow itself to be forced to do anything, because it rests upon a decision by Christ Himself to devote Himself to this particular person in a particular situation. The reasons for this free decision are not objects of human judgement.

In as far as the conscious choice for Christ is placed in man's freedom, the possibility certainly exists that this experience can pass by almost unnoticed, a fact which Rudolf Steiner repeatedly pointed to with anxiety.[112] With the end of Kali Yuga, 1899, mankind grew into the reality of the spiritual world. Man lived in this reality in its hidden, unconscious depths, but this indwelling can only be a blessing if it becomes conscious. That is the task which was not taken up in the first century of the Age of Light, and has thus become a tragedy. The Christ Event consists, among other things, of the fact that Christ Himself has come as close to humanity as possible. With His appearance in the etheric world He has approached mankind from the realm of the spirit, as closely as He can possibly get to the Threshold without entering the physical-material world once again. One of His messages of farewell, however, was: 'My Kingdom is not of this World.' In so far as the experience of Christ is concerned, the innumerable ways in which He can make His appearance are always supersensible.

A prerequisite for man of the twentieth century to find the Christ Event in his individual consciousness was the Christ Sacrifice of the nineteenth century. This Christ Sacrifice, which signifies a Crucifixion, was necessitated by the materialistic consciousness which was carried into the spiritual world by the dead in past centuries. Christ, in the figure of an Angel, lost His spiritual consciousness, and 'the lack of consciousness which befell Christ in the spiritual world... will become the awakening of the Christ-Consciousness in the souls of people on earth between birth and death in the twentieth century'.[113] This awakening to consciousness, however, is dependent upon the fact that the Resurrection-Body of Christ has evolved, developed and grown so much stronger since the time of the Mystery of Golgotha that it is able to reproduce Itself in a growth-process which can make Itself available to a larger number of people. This process counteracts the 'kink', the 'thorn in the flesh' which comes from Sorath and fixes human consciousness on earthly objects. Against this, a reversal takes place which counteracts it within the human being.

And to this is added the fact that, through reincarnation, an ever greater number of people bring with them what they have acquired from the Christ-impulse in one—or two—post-Christian lives, and which they have worked on in the spiritual world.[114] For, due to the opposition of physical-material nature, man can only take up a germinal amount of the Christ-impulse in a single lifetime. After death this germ continues to grow, so that, in descending to a new life, it flows into the whole of man's being. This process is not unique; it is repeated in every incarnation and leads to a gradual comprehension of the Christ Being who approaches mankind.

The Christ Event, in the first place, can be found in the appearance of anthroposophy in the twentieth century. All the preparatory conditions mentioned must have been met for this occurrence to take place. With that a kind of paradox is again evident. Anthroposophy prepares for this event which, in another guise, is the happening itself. And it can only make its appearance when the possibility has been thoroughly prepared in the human constitution by consciously accepting a spiritual content into thinking. Connected with that is the principle of understanding anthroposophy, a thing which is often emphasized by Rudolf Steiner. The ideas and thoughts of anthroposophy are fully capable of being understood by an impartial and developing thinking, which includes a gradual penetration of thinking, feeling and willing. Spiritual science places man, as a sensible, enquiring, responsible being into the spiritual world. It is only this expanded scientific consciousness which guarantees his presence there in a humanly worthy form. Whoever, in his understanding of spiritual contents, does not notice the subtle process that frees him in a delicate way from his material bodily nature misses an experience which occurs, to begin with, at the boundary of his consciousness. Through careful attention this experience can be raised into consciousness in such a way that the etheric process, which actually underlies such comprehension, can be consciously grasped. With that an inner fact comes to mind, which is an essential characteristic of the twentieth century and one which shows how consciousness is beginning to change. Certainly this experience is delicate and fleeting and is quickly forgotten, so that the etheric process involved in understanding anthroposophy is very easily overlooked in the life of the soul. That can go so far that, in retrospect, the comprehension itself can be doubted. On the positive side, however, it means that the comprehension of anthroposophy requires an etheric activity in which the ego is present as long as this continues. In a certain sense it loses its reality if the process no longer really takes place. One is not supported by what has already taken place; it has to be repeated in order to become real.

The understanding of anthroposophy can be endlessly deepened; it knows all degrees. If the understanding of the experience in the etheric is strengthened, it can become a vessel for the manifestation of the Etheric Christ. Rudolf Steiner once said in a Christmas lecture, speaking about the new understanding of the Christ which comes from anthroposophy, that it was the Child which would 'grow up so that the Etheric Christ would incarnate into it, just as Christ was able to incarnate in the flesh at the time of the Mystery of Golgotha'.[115] To deepen our understanding of anthroposophy until we can experience this Child, in which the new and best powers of mankind are united, is a task whose fulfilment prepares a vessel for the Etheric Christ.

The fact that anthroposophy is built upon the supersensible Christ Event is nowhere to be experienced more strongly than at the laying of the Foundation Stone at Christmas 1923. Already at the laying of the Foundation Stone for the Goetheanum in September 1913 this is recognizable through the fact that Rudolf Steiner spoke the 'macrocosmic World Prayer' for the first time and passed it on to others. This 'macrocosmic World Prayer', the 'reversed Lord's Prayer', was spoken in private by Jesus of Nazareth as He prepared for and awaited the incarnation of Christ. Now, in 1913, when it was no longer a question of incarnation but one of etherization, it flowed into the building-impulse of the Goetheanum, in which a powerful force of spiritualization dwelt, which releases matter—that is, etherealizes it. This impulse emerged again in a changed and intensified form at the laying of the Foundation Stone at Christmas 1923. The soul of man calls itself through the spirit to its most noble work of exercising willing, feeling and thinking, which are bound up in the threefold nature of man to the spirituality of the world. The doing of exercises leads into the Christ-sphere, to the truth of thinking, feeling and willing. Through that the fundamental truth of the

Trinity and the Hierarchies who serve it can be revealed. The three truths —

From God mankind has being
In Christ, death becomes life
In the spirit's universal thoughts the soul awakens —

which express the relationship of the Trinity to man, are heard already by the elemental beings in the etheric realms. It is up to human beings to hear them too. This acceptance of a supersensible happening through an inner perception of the spirit-call to mankind demands an understanding which simultaneously takes conscious hold of the etheric. The Foundation Stone lives in the etheric realm, in the Christ-sphere to which man can raise himself in genuine understanding. The Foundation Stone — like the Grail — is the vessel in which the Etheric Christ can appear.

The Etheric Christ Event can be found and experienced directly in the fourth part of the Foundation Stone; light and warmth, as etheric qualities, illumine and warm head and heart. This fourth section of the Foundation Stone is both the source and the aim of the spiritual Event. But here, too, as always, the rule applies that the work of the ego can only perform a part of the task. The other part lies beyond the Threshold in the etheric realm, which inclines towards the ego in grace and freedom.[116]

A quite different way to seek and gain access to the Christ Event is given by those processes in time mentioned above, which provide mankind with the impression of doom, of confronting the abyss, the void. This more or less conscious experience of what — in a certain sense — is the true situation of the time, releases all the feelings of desperation, fear and hate which countless of our fellow human beings know only too well from their own experience. People, quite understandably, try to protect themselves from these half-conscious, or unconscious, almost unbearable soul-experiences, by diversion, intoxication or flight. In view of this soul-occasioned flight-tendency a change of direction, a true conversion, like a Damascus experience, is necessary. At some time or other a person must become aware of the fact that, in so far as his own experience goes, he simultaneously turns away from that which gives spiritual meaning to the present age. A man must endure a kind of Damascus experience in order to find the strength to bear what is otherwise unendurable. By enduring what is terrible, frightening, fear-inspiring, the picture gradually changes. One becomes aware of a serious, searching gaze which calls one to self-knowledge, penetrating and imbuing one with courage. If a person has studied anthroposophy, then it will be clear to him that all that he has studied, all that he has striven for, has been a preparation for this moment of probation. The whole of anthroposophy will be experienced as a preparation for the meeting with the Guardian; it will help him to come into the right relationship to the Guardian of the Threshold. It will be clear to him that the Spirits who create, bear, and bestow grace on humanity live in the trinity and that the human being who wishes to unite with them must consciously place himself, with his threefold organism, into the trinity of the world. Only in this way can the Guardian of the Threshold, who may appear externally as an enemy of mankind but is really man's friend, allow him to enter the spiritual world. Through this standing within the threefoldness that comes into being through the living thinking of the three entities, man further becomes aware of the fact that Michael, as an Archai Spirit, is the one who bears into the world the divine principle of threefoldness, through courage, enthusiasm and love, because the evil powers are thereby checked. The impulses of anthroposophy to acknowledge man as a threefold being, to penetrate the social organism with the Threefold Order, in order to overcome force, have their roots here in the Being of Michael; here are all the sources of their nourishment.

Only when man has become imbued with this principle of threefoldness, borne through the world by Michael, will the Michael Being reveal to him the Christ Appearance at the present day. This is at the same time both deeply hidden in the spirit and quite close to man in all his needs. The War of All against All, which continually threatens to gain prevalence, is nothing else than the great shadow cast by the spiritual events standing in the background of earthly happenings. The events of the hour themselves drive mankind, so to speak, in all branches of life, towards the Threshold of the spiritual world. The trial of mankind in this sense consists of finding the way towards the Christ Event of the present day, by recognizing the spiritual nature of this process.

The changed position of Christ towards humanity, His approach in the etheric, creates new types of experience. Two processes, which can be spontaneously experienced, allow man to participate in the etheric Christ Event. The necessary happenings descend from the etheric world, prepare themselves there a few days in advance and can be received as a kind of premonition.

Everything a person does requires karmic recompense. The impulse for this recompense is engendered simultaneously and in secret for the destined compensatory deed to be produced later. When Christ inscribed the guilt of the adultress into the earth, it was the archetypal portrayal of this process. It is now possible again for people to experience this process briefly, like the casting of a shadow.

These and other similar experiences are the harbingers of a new natural clairvoyance, which will develop further in the future.[117]

To conclude let me mention three forms in which Christ can appear to man — though these also contain within themselves an endless multiplicity.

To many people in this century Christ has appeared as an Angel, as a Helper, as a Saviour, as a Comforter. Reliable witness has been given to this fact. There are more experiences of this than there are witnesses, partly because of a justified reticence to speak about such things, or even to write about them; partly, also, because the experience has withdrawn from the consciousness in retrospect. Forgetfulness easily occurs in the case of supersensible experiences. It is noteworthy that interventions in people's lives, right down to the physical level, although remembered as an act of grace and also by the fact that a certain religious mood is left behind, are not further worked on by the people concerned in their present life—at least as far as that takes place in public.

Another, quite opposite, character is shown in Damascus experiences. Ultimately every human being in the course of his incarnations must experience a meeting with the Christ, which affects him so deeply in his ego that it leads to a turning-point, to a conversion in his whole subsequent life, as happened for example when Saul became Paul. The Damascus experience is preceded by a rejection, a feeling of reserve or opposition towards the Christ-impulse. The development which results from that has to come to a crisis through which the Damascus experience is prepared in the depths of the soul. For what appears as a flash of lightning out of a clear sky has really been well prepared in order to bear fruit. Through a Damascus experience an intensive connection of the ego to Christ takes place, which develops further into the future. Such a meeting is impressed deeply into the consciousness. In its characteristics the Damascus meeting corresponds exactly with the development of consciousness and personality. It is therefore a question as to why there is so little mention of such meetings. Is it the result of the great reserve which a person imposes on himself in the face of such an experience?

The moment in life when a person meets anthroposophy so that it makes a lasting impression on him, and continues to do so throughout his whole life, bears a certain relationship to a Damascus experience, just because a karmic situation is brought about which in itself leads back to events in a previous life.

The third form in which Christ encounters people has come about through the fact that Christ has taken over the role of Judge for the karma of all mankind, which was earlier administered by Moses for those who had built up a connection with it in life. Man encounters this Karmic Judge at various stages in the life after death, so that a growing consciousness of karma can thereby arise in one's next life. This will take effect more and more upon the deeds which have to be performed and upon the future. This process, which starts in the twentieth century and will occupy the next three thousand years, also stands in connection with the Christ Event, which takes place in the etheric realm and will become increasingly evident to man.

This office will be transferred in the course of our time — and that is the important point — to Christ Jesus, and man will encounter Christ Jesus more and more as his Judge, as his Karmic Judge. That is the supersensible event. In exactly the same way as the Event in Palestine took place at the beginning of our era on the physical plane, so will the office of the Karmic Judge be handed on to Christ Jesus in our age in the next higher realm. And it is this fact which works in such a way into the physical world, on the physical plane, that mankind will evolve a feeling of this kind: in everything he does, he performs a deed for which he will have to be accountable to Christ. And this feeling, which will occur in a perfectly natural way in the course of mankind's evolution, will change its form, so that the soul will become suffused with Light, which will gradually come to radiate from man himself and will illuminate the Christ Figure within the etheric world. And the more this feeling, which will have a more lofty significance than abstract conscience, develops, the more will the etheric Figure of Christ become visible during the next centuries.[118]

What Rudolf Steiner expressed in these words was felt as a premonition by Friedrich Hebbel, when he combined the closeness, the healing and the love of Christ in the words which I will conclude with:

And from His darkest places
The Lord steps forth amain[119]
And the threads which had been severed
He knots them up again.[120]

# Notes

GA = *Gesamtausgabe*, collected works of Rudolf Steiner in the original German. Published translations are available via Rudolf Steiner Press, London, and Anthroposophic Press, New York. Unpublished typescripts referred to are from the Rudolf Steiner House Library, London.

1 From a lecture by Rudolf Steiner to the priests of the Christian Community, September 1924, cited by Harold Giersch: *Rudolf Steiner über die Wiederkunft Christi* [Concerning the reappearance of Christ], Dornach 1991, p. 110. [In order to elucidate these statements about the comets see: 'Earth and Stars', lecture to workmen, 20 September 1924, typescript R 75, where it is explained that the prediction of the collision of Biela's Comet with the earth in 1933 did not derive from Rudolf Steiner, but was the prediction of the astronomer Littrow (1781–1840), and that already in 1852 the comet had split up and did not cause the predicted devastation — Translator's note.]
2 Rudolf Steiner, lecture to the workmen at the Goetheanum, GA 351, 24 October 1923.
3 See note 1, lecture to the priests.
4 Alfred Heidenreich: *Die Erscheinung des Christus in der ätherischen Welt* [The appearance of the Christ in the etheric world], Dornach 1990, p.31ff.
5 See in this connection the article in the 1996 New Year's edition of *Der Spiegel*: 'Endzeit Angst' [Doomsday terror].
6 Without any claim to completeness—
J. Ben-Aharon: *The Spiritual Event of the Twentieth Century*, London 1993;
K. Heyer: *Wesen und Wollen des Nationalsozialismus*, Basel 1991;
C. Lindenberg: *Die Technik des Bösen*, Stuttgart 1978;
C. Lindenberg: *Vom geistigen Ursprung der Gegenwart*, Stuttgart 1984;
H.W. Schroeder: *Der Mensch und das Böse*, Stuttgart 1984;

J. Tautz: *Der Eingriff des Widersachers. Fragen zum okkulten Aspekt des Nationalsocialismus*, Freiburg in Breisgau 1976; T. Stöckli (Editor): *Wege zur Christus-Erfahrung*, Dornach 1991.

7 Rudolf Steiner: *From Symptom to Reality in Modern History*, lecture 4, Rudolf Steiner Press 1976, p. 112.
8 Rudolf Steiner: GA 110, answers to questions, 21 April 1909 in Düsseldorf (not included in English edition, *The Spiritual Hierarchies and their Reflection in the Physical World*).
9 Ibid. See also Rudolf Steiner: *Theosophy of the Rosicrucian*, Rudolf Steiner Press 1966, lecture of 2 June 1907 in Munich.
10 *The Deed of Christ and the Opposing Spiritual Powers, Lucifer, Ahriman, Mephistopheles, Asuras*, Steiner Book Centre 1976, lecture 22 March 1909 in Berlin.
11 See note 8. Answers to questions, 21 April 1909 in Düsseldorf.
12 See particularly in this connection Rudolf Steiner's *Occult Science*, Rudolf Steiner Press 1979, chapter headed: 'The Character of Occult Science'.
13 Rudolf Steiner: *The Apocalypse of St John*, Rudolf Steiner Press 1977. See also: H. W. Schroeder, 'Sorat und das Jahrhundertende', *Mitteilungen aus der Anthroposophischen Arbeit in Deutschland*, Michaelmas 1979.
14 *Three Streams in the Evolution of Mankind*, Rudolf Steiner Press 1965, lectures of 11, 12, 13 October 1918 in Dornach.
15 See note 13. Lecture of 29 June 1908 in Nuremberg.
16 Ibid.
17 Ibid.
18 Ibid.
19 Ibid.
20 Ibid.
21 Ibid.
22 Ibid.
23 Ibid.
24 Ibid.
25 'How do I Find the Christ' in *Evil*, Rudilf Steiner Press 1997, lecture of 16 October 1918.
26 Ibid.
27 See note 14. Lecture 11 October 1918.

28 In this connection see also Christoph Lindenberg: *Vom geistigen Ursprung der Gegenwart* [Concerning the spiritual origin of the present day], Stuttgart 1984.
29 See note 14. Lecture of 11 October 1918.
30 Ibid., lecture of 12 October 1918 in Dornach.
31 Ibid., lecture of 12 October 1918 in Dornach.
32 Ibid., lecture of 11 October 1918 in Dornach.
33 Ibid., lecture of 12 October 1918 in Dornach.
34 Peter Tradowsky: *Kaspar Hauser*, London 1997.
35 Guido Knopp: *Hitler – eine Bilanz*, Berlin 1995.
36 Rudolf Steiner: *Towards Social Renewal*, Rudolf Steiner Press 1977, Appendix, 'To the German Nation and the Civilized World'.
37 See note 36.
38 Ibid.
39 Ibid.
40 Ibid.
41 Rudolf Steiner: GA 195, lecture of 1 January 1920, Stuttgart, in which he refers to his essay of 1888, 'Die geistige Signatur der Gegenwart'.
42 Quoted from Rudolf Steiner: *Das Schicksalsjahr 1923 in der Geschichte der Anthroposophischen Gesellschaft* [The year of destiny 1923 in the history of the Anthroposophical Society], GA 259.
43 Let us here be reminded of the fact that a similar movement working in this direction made itself felt in Russia after 1917. See in this connection Rudolf Steiner: *Polarities in the Evolution of Mankind*, Rudolf Steiner Press 1987, pp. 43–44, lecture of 13 June 1920, Stuttgart. 'Leninism knows how to put things cleverly, using rational ideas produced in the head, and there is a definite reason for this. The cleverness of the human animal, the cleverness of human animal nature, is coming to the fore in human evolution through Leninism. Everything arising from human instincts, human selfishness, comes to interpretation in Leninism and Trotskyism in a form that on the surface seems very intelligent. The human animal wants to work its way to the fore, to be the most intelligent of animals. All the ahrimanic powers that aim to exclude the human element, to exclude everything that is specifically

human, and all the aptitudes that exist within the animal kingdom are to become the forces that determine humanity ... If you now take all the cleverness of this kind that exists within the whole animal kingdom, and imagine ahrimanic powers taking this up and making it come to life in human instincts, you can see that it may be true to say that Lenin, Trotsky and others are the tools of those ahrimanic powers. That is an ahrimanic initiation. It belongs to a different cosmic sphere than our own world does. It is however an initiation that also holds the potential for getting rid of human civilization on earth, getting rid of everything that has evolved by way of human civilization.'

The cleverness of the human animal that leads to the ahrimanic initiation cannot easily be compared with the power of the apocalyptic Beast. Nevertheless a close connection cannot be overlooked. For the 'thorn' which the activity of Sorath has left behind in the human physical body exists in the same sphere as the human instinct, human egoism, which was mentioned in the lecture. As regards the later activity of Stalin one must at least wonder whether the forces of Sorath are not continually increasing in strength. One is reminded for instance of the persecution of the Kulaks in the twenties, of the purges of the thirties, in which Stalin liquidated more that 1 million party members, and of many other things too.

44 According to the facsimile of the Memorial to the German Resistance Movement in the Berlin Zoo.
45 Peter Tradowsky: *Ere the Century Closes*, Whitby 1995.
46 Karl Heyer (noted during Nazi times, written 1945): *Wenn die Götter den Tempel verlassen* [When the Gods forsake the temple], Freiburg im Breisgau 1947; *Der Staat als Werkzeug des Bösen* [The state as tool of the evil one], Stuttgart 1965; *Wesen und Wollen des National Sozialismus* [Character and aim of National Socialism], Basel 1991.
47 See note 35.
48 Michaelis & Schraepler: *Ursachen und Folgen* [Causes and effects], vol. xxiv, Berlin (no date).
49 Ibid.
50 Ibid.

## NOTES

51 Ibid.
52 Ibid.
53 Hitler: *Mein Kampf*.
54 See note 35, p. 59f.
55 See note 41.
56 See note 35, p. 58.
57 Ibid., p. 60.
58 Ibid., p. 66.
59 Rudolf Steiner: *From Jesus to Christ*, Rudolf Steiner Press 1973, lecture of 5 October 1911 in Karlsruhe.
60 Ibid.
61 Ibid.
62 Ibid.
63 See note 45.
64 Rudolf Steiner: *Mensch und Welt. Das Wirken des Geistes in der Natur. Über das Wesen der Bienen* [Man and the universe. The activity of the spirit in nature. Lectures on bees], GA 351, 10 October 1923 in Dornach.
65 This idea is quite briefly mentioned in the book *Ere the Century Closes*. See note 45.
66 Rudolf Steiner: *Menschenwerden, Weltenseele und Weltengeist* [Human development, World Soul and World-Spirit] GA 206, Part II, lecture of 6 August 1921 in Dornach ('The remedy of our diseased civilization'). Rudolf Steiner speaks here of ahrimanic powers. If one takes the above lectures into consideration they appear to be identical with what he says about Sorath, or to have a close connection.
67 Ibid.
68 Ibid.
69 'The Work of the Angels in Our Astral Body', lecture of 9 October 1918 in Zürich, in *Angels*, Rudolf Steiner Press 1996.
70 Ibid.
71 Rudolf Steiner: *Mysterien Wahrheiten and Weihnachtsimpulse*, lecture of 23 December 1917 in Basel, 'Et incarnatus est', GA 180.
72 Peter Tradowsky: *Kaspar Hauser*. See note 34.
73 See note 71, lecture of 26 December 1917: '... everything which lies along this path belongs to the realm of the truly effective results of what happens after 33 years. And then,

when a seed such as this has, as it were, been sown, has matured, it continues to be active. A human generation of 33 years ripens as a thought-germ, a germ of action. Once it has ripened it works on for another 66 years into history. One can also recognize the intensity of an impulse which a person implants into history in its effect over three generations, throughout a whole century'.
74 See note 59.
75 Rudolf Steiner: lecture of 8 August 1920 in Dornach, 'Die Zwölf Sinne des Menschen in ihrer Beziehung zu Imagination, Inspiration und Intuition' [The twelve senses of man in their connection to Imagination, Inspiration and Intuition], GA 199.
76 See especially in this connection: *The Foundations of Human Experience*, Anthroposophic Press 1996, GA 293, lecture of 4 September 1919 in Stuttgart.
77 From the verse written for the Berlin friends.
78 See note 36, chapter 1.
79 Ibid.
80 Ibid.
81 Ibid.
82 Rudolf Steiner: *Polarities in the Evolution of Mankind*, Rudolf Steiner Press 1987, lecture of 14 November 1920 in Stuttgart.
83 Ibid., lecture of 22 November 1920 in Stuttgart.
84 Ibid.
85 Rudolf Steiner: lecture of 25 December 1920 in Dornach. From GA 202. Translated in *Anthroposophical Quarterly*, 18, No. 4.
86 *Beiträge zur Rudolf Steiner Gesamtausgabe*, Nos. 67/68, '1879–1979—Hundert Jahre Michael-Zeitalter' (Michaelmas 1979). Earliest detailed account by Rudolf Steiner of the Michael Event of 1879, Munich, 5 December 1907. For other aspects see note 45.
87 See note 45, p. 59f.
88 On the question of money, see note 36, Chapter 3: 'Capitalism and Social Ideas (Capital and Human Labour)'. Dieter Suhr: *Alterndes Geld* [Ageing money], Schaffhausen 1988.
Margrit Kennedy: *Geld ohne Zinsen und Inflation* [Money without interest and inflation], München 1991.

NOTES 107

89 See note 13, lecture of 24 June 1908 in Nuremberg.
90 Wilhelm Pelikan: *Der Halleysche Komet* [Halley's Comet], Dornach 1985.
91 Rudolf Steiner: lecture in Stuttgart on 13 March 1910, 'Comets and their significance for earthly existence', in *Anthroposophical News Sheet*, 246.
92 Rudolf Steiner: lecture in Munich, 13 March 1910.
93 See Rudolf Steiner: *The Christ Impulse and the Development of Ego Consciousness*, Anthroposophic Press 1976, lecture of 9 March 1910.
'Thus humanity is now called upon to make a decision, whether it shall allow itself, through what comes with Halley's Comet, to be led down into a darkness even lower than that of Kali Yuga, or whether through an understanding developed by anthroposophy it will not neglect to cultivate the new faculties by which it may find the way to the land which, according to Eastern Literature, has disappeared, but which Christ will once more reveal to mankind—the land of Shamballa. That is the question of the dividing of the ways: either to go down or to go up. Either to go down into something which as a Cosmic Kamaloka lies still deeper down than Kali-Yuga, or to work for that which will enable man to enter that realm which is really alluded to under the name of Shamballa'. This statement is applicable to the year 1910, but can also apply to 1986.
94 Vladimir Solovyev: *The Antichrist*, Edinburgh 1982.
95 Ibid.
96 H.P. van Manen: *Das Goetheanum*, 3 March 1996.
97 Ibid.
98 Rudolf Steiner: *The Influences of Lucifer and Ahriman*, Anthroposophic Press 1993, lecture of 1 November 1919 in Dornach.
99 Ibid., lecture of 2 November 1919 in Dornach.
100 Rudolf Steiner: GA 193, lecture of 27 October 1919, Zürich.
101 Rudolf Steiner: *The Influences of Lucifer and Ahriman*, lecture from 4 November 1919 in Berne.
102 See note 25.
103 Helmuth James Graf von Moltke, *Briefe an Freya* [Letters to Freya]

Albrecht Haushofer, *Moabiter Sonette* [Moabite Sonnets].
Ken Saro-Wiwa, over 30 titles currently available in English.
104 See note 25. 'How do I find the Christ?', lecture of 16 October 1918 in Zürich, GA 182.
105 Ibid.
106 Ibid.
107 Ibid.
108 Lecture of 9 October 1918 in Zürich, see note 69.
109 See *Occult Science*, Chapter V, 'Knowledge of Higher Worlds. Concerning Initiation.'
110 Rudolf Steiner: *The Christmas Conference*, Anthroposophic Press 1990, the Foundation Meeting of 25 December.
111 Rudolf Steiner: *The New Spirituality and the Christ Experience of the Twentieth Century*, Rudolf Steiner Press 1988, lectures of 23–31 October, 1920, Dornach.
112 See note 91.
113 Rudolf Steiner: GA152, lecture of 2 May 1913 in London. See also note 45.
114 See note 12, Chapter IV, 'Man and the Evolution of the World'.
115 Lecture of 26 December 1914 in Dornach, GA 156.
116 See in this connection:
F.W. Zeylmans van Emichoven: *The Foundation Stone*, London 1963.
Rudolf Grosse: *The Christmas Conference; Beginning of a New Cosmic Age*, N. Vancouver 1984.
Peter Tradowsky: *Ere the Century Closes*, Whitby 1995.
Peter Tradowsky: *Johannes der Täufer und Lazarus-Johannes* [John the Baptist and Lazaras-John], Dornach 1995.
117 See note 91.
118 *From Jesus to Christ*, Rudolf Steiner Press 1991, lecture of 7 October 1911 in Karlsruhe.
119 'Amain' (archaic), meaning 'with force'.
120 Friedrich Hebbel from his poem: 'Die Weihe der Nacht' ['The Consecration of Night'].